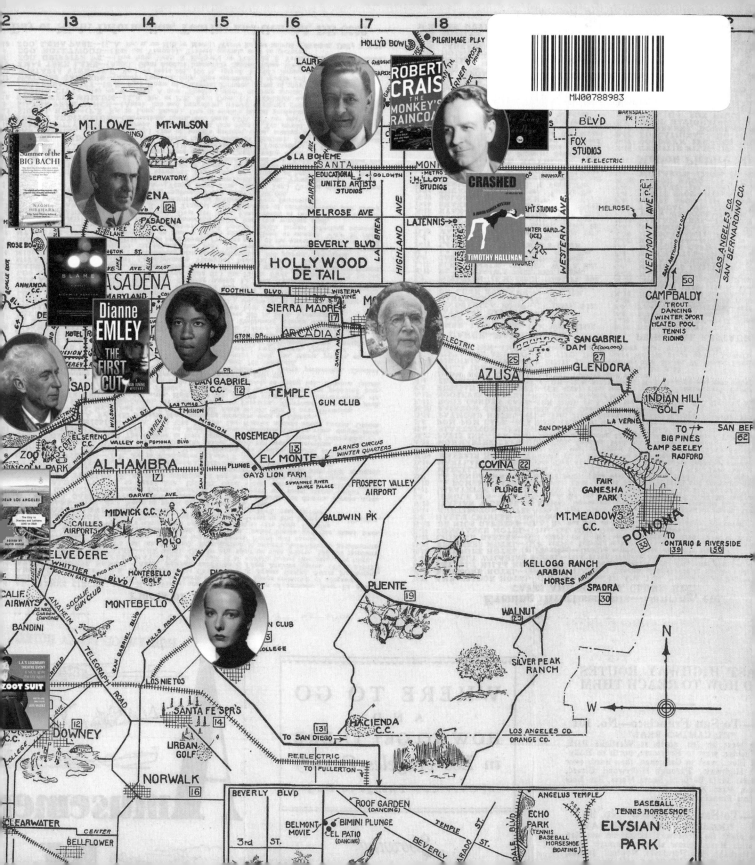

MW00788983

A "READ TO INSPIRE MORE
READING DURING QUARANTINE
COVID-19 2020

HAPPY FATHERS
DAY !

READ ME, LOS ANGELES

EXPLORING L.A.'S BOOK CULTURE

KATIE ORPHAN

EDITED BY COLLEEN DUNN BATES,
WITH KATELYN KEATING & JULIANNE JOHNSON

Prospect Park Books

Essays © 2020 by Katie Orphan
Original photographs © 2020 by Shahin Ansari

All rights reserved. No part of this book may be reproduced or transmitted in any form or by any means, electronic or mechanical, including photocopying, recording, or by any information storage and retrieval system, without permission in writing from the publisher.

 Published by Prospect Park Books
2359 Lincoln Avenue
Altadena, California 91001
www.prospectparkbooks.com

Distributed by Consortium Books Sales & Distribution
www.cbsd.com

Library of Congress Cataloging in Publication Data
Names: Orphan, Katie, author. | Dunn Bates, Colleen, author. | Johnson, Julianne author. | Keating, Katelyn author.
Title: Read me, Los Angeles : exploring L.A.'s book culture / Katie Orphan ; with Colleen Dunn Bates, Julianne Johnson & Katelyn Keating.
Other titles: Read me, L.A.
Identifiers: LCCN 2019034200 | ISBN 9781945551680 (hardcover) | ISBN 9781945551697 (epub)
Subjects: LCSH: Los Angeles (Calif.)--Guidebooks. | Literary landmarks--California--Los Angeles--Guidebooks. | Novelists, American--Homes and haunts--California--Los Angeles--Guidebooks. | Los Angeles (Calif.)--Intellectual life--Guidebooks. | Los Angeles (Calif.)--In literature.
Classification: LCC F869.L83 O77 2020 | DDC 917.94/94--dc23
LC record available at https://lccn.loc.gov/2019034200

Edited by Colleen Dunn Bates
Contributions by Katelyn Keating & Julianne Johnson
Original photographs by Shahin Ansari
Cover illustration by Kate Wong
Designed by Amy Inouye, Future Studio

Image permissions: Page 76, Julia Child image, photograph & related rights™ © 2019, The Julia Child Foundation for Gastronomy and the Culinary Arts. Page 86, "City in Mind: A Lyrical Map of the Concept of Los Angeles" 2011, by J Michael Walker; color pencil on polypropylene paper, 60" high x 276" wide; courtesy the Special Collections Library of the University of California. Page 167, photo of Lummis House & Garden courtesy of Los Angeles City Parks. Other photo credits as noted throughout the book. All other photos by Shahin Ansari.

Text permissions: Page 46, "The Beach at Sunset" by Eloise Klein Healy, granted by Red Hen Press. Page 50, "Love Poem to Los Angeles," granted by Luis Rodriguez. Page 60, "Los Angeles," granted by Kamau Daáood. Page 114, "LA Authors," granted by Mike Sonksen.

First edition, first printing
Printed in China

To love L.A. is to love more than a city.
It's to love a language.

— WANDA COLEMAN, *Native in a Strange Land* (1997)

CONTENTS

FOREWORD
MY KIND OF TOWN
COLLEEN DUNN BATES

NEIL SIMON ONCE SAID that L.A. was "like paradise with a lobotomy." To that, I say, with full respect to the late great writer: Screw you. If you had ever explored beyond the boundaries of the Beverly Hills Hotel, Mr. Simon, you would have found a real city full of real people, plenty of whom are smart and thoughtful and diverse and complicated. In short, people who read books.

I grew up a reader in Los Angeles in the '60s and '70s, regularly walking barefoot to the Hillhurst Library in Los Feliz to get another stack of preteen mysteries. A few years later, the Immaculate Heart nuns helped me fall in love with Steinbeck and Salinger and Hurston. My mother, also a native, found refuge from her pack of children by reading Fitzgerald and Fowles; my father, also a native, has always loved some rollicking Donald Westlake and Walter Mosley.

My family was not unusual. From the days of Helen Hunt Jackson and Charles Fletcher Lummis, my city has always been literary. L.A. hosts the nation's largest book festival. Our main library is so extraordinary that Susan Orlean wrote the bestselling *The Library Book* about it. We're home to a few dozen publishing companies, including mine, a rich array of bookstores, more literary agents than you might think, and enough readings, poetry slams, writing workshops, book clubs, and festivals to keep readers and writers happy 365 days a year. Yes, our book culture is overshadowed by the entertainment industry, but guess where many of the best productions on Netflix come from? That's right: books.

Because of all this, I'd been scheming on publishing a book about L.A.'s literary culture for years, but it simmered on a back burner. Then one day in late 2018, something snapped when I read Elina Shatkin's hilarious takedown on LAist.com of yet another clueless *New York Times* piece about Los Angeles. It was time.

I asked a few bookseller friends what they thought about the idea, and lo and behold, Katie Orphan, who at the time was managing the Last Bookstore, said she'd been working on a proposal for a very similar book and her agent (L.A.'s own Dara Hyde) was just about to submit it to me. Kismet! The bookseller and the publisher joined forces, and I built a team of Angelenos to help create our dream book about L.A. and its books: designer Amy Inouye; photographer Shahin Ansari; Prospect Park editors Katelyn Keating and Julianne Johnson; and freelance editors Leilah Bernstein and Margery Schwartz. Six of this group of eight are natives. So much for the trope that nobody is actually from L.A., which is as big a myth as the one about nobody walking in L.A. Or nobody reading.

We chose to structure this book as loosely as the city is structured, to foster a sense of discovery and delight. You can dive in anywhere and look for something that catches your fancy. Join Katie having coffee with Michael Connelly in DTLA, or remembering Octavia E. Butler in Pasadena, or showcasing the strong YA book culture. Explore the bookstores and libraries and literary-rooted bars. Get inspired to volunteer at 826LA or WriteGirl. Put next year's LATFOB and LitFest on your calendar. Pick through our lists of must-read L.A. books, and get irritated if we neglected your favorite. Enjoy quotes galore from writers galore.

Most of all, our biggest hope is that *Read Me, Los Angeles* adds depth, richness, and just plain fun to your L.A. experience, whether you're a native like me or a first-time visitor. Read all about it, Los Angeles.

Finally, it was the city that held us, the city they said had no center, that all of us had come to from all over America because this was the place to find dreams and pleasure and love.

— CAROLYN SEE, *Golden Days* (1986)

NEWCOMERS TO L.A.

I felt new here,
and the sheer breadth
of Los Angeles still
astonished me. It seemed
like I could drive and
drive and the city would
just keep unfurling,
as if it were a map of
Los Angeles being
unrolled as I drove over
it, rather than a city
that started and stopped
somewhere specific.

— SUSAN ORLEAN,
The Library Book (2018)

Now I was truly in 'God's country'—the real
Southern California, which is peerless....
Next day, February 1, 1885, a thirty-mile walk
through beautiful towns, past the picturesque old
Mission San Gabriel, and down a matchless
valley, brought me at midnight to my unknown
home in the City of Angels.

— CHARLES FLETCHER LUMMIS,
A Tramp Across the Continent (1892)

Life in Los Angeles is not as toxic as in
New York. The proximity of the Orient and
to Mexico has made people less obsessionally
ambitious and more in love with life. Everyone
has a garden, and people are not enslaved by the
clock.... You feel the fruitfulness of the canyons,
and the presence of the sea. The sun pulls you out
of the house.

— ANAÏS NIN,
The Diary of Anaïs Nin 1947-1955 (1974)

THE BIG SHOW
MICHAEL CONNELLY

MICHAEL CONNELLY TOOK TIME away from the writers' room of *Bosch*, the Amazon series based on his best-selling Harry Bosch detective novels, to meet for coffee near the downtown courthouses and LAPD headquarters that have made their way into his many novels. We settled at a communal table, and he went from writing about intense interrogations to being the subject of a very mild one.

Originally from Florida, Connelly moved to L.A. for a job at the *Los Angeles Times*. Seeking work at the *Times* was born out of a desire to write crime novels; he was looking for a place to live and work that would serve as a location for his fiction. "My three favorite writers and biggest influences wrote about L.A. and Southern California," he said. "Even though I'd applied for jobs in other cities, my hope was that I'd end up in L.A. I'd never even been to California until I came here to interview at newspapers."

Those three favorite authors are, perhaps not surprisingly, Raymond Chandler, Ross Macdonald, and Joseph Wambaugh. "Three different generations or eras of crime fiction," Connelly said. "I really loved those private-eye, outsider stories. I discovered Raymond Chandler in college—it was the right age, when you feel like an outsider. Then Wambaugh wrote about detectives in the LAPD, and that was an interesting change for me. I became a journalist and had that 'in' as well. It was that adage, write what you know, and I knew more about police detectives than private detectives."

Connelly said the transition from being a journalist to a fiction writer wasn't much of a challenge: "I wanted to do that first. It was my father's idea. He said, 'If you go down the road of being an English major, you'll be a teacher. If you want to write crime novels, maybe you should be a journalist and get in courtrooms and police stations.'"

Mark DeLong Photography

The setting sun burned the sky pink and orange in the same bright hues as surfers' bathing suits. It was beautiful deception, Bosch thought, as he drove north on the Hollywood Freeway to home. Sunsets did that here. Made you forget it was the smog that made their colors so brilliant, that behind every pretty picture there could be an ugly story.

— Michael Connelly,
The Black Echo (1992)

Reporting about the LAPD influenced Connelly's understanding of their procedures and helped refine the accuracy of his representations. "I haven't been a journalist since 1994, but I covered the LAPD for seven years," he explained. "Obviously, the LAPD of '87 or '94 was a lot different from today, so I've always maintained connections and built new ones. I write about fictional detectives, but I try to make their world real."

That world is a grounded, well-described Los Angeles, with details that let locals recognize their home and allow readers elsewhere to understand more about the city than the clichés. There are several factors, including his past as a journalist, that have helped Connelly get things right. "I still feel like I write like a journalist," he said. "I go to the places I write about and get details that make them interesting, at least to me. If you plant the feet of your character in the real world, it empathically connects them to the reader."

Along with the successful TV series, two movies have been made based on his books—*Blood Work* and *The Lincoln Lawyer*. "Movies are different from TV," Connelly said. "They don't want the author involved. What you can control is who you sell the book to, and because both of those were considered high-concept films, I had choices on who to give them to. I had all the control at first, and then I had none once I made that decision. I think I chose well. Both were a thrill. You write in a room by yourself, and then you get to see them come to life in that way.

"TV is way different. It's a writer's medium. Amazon came to me and said, 'Let's make a TV show,' and I said the only way I'll do it is if I get to pick the guy and we don't farm it out—it has to be made in L.A. I built the book

The Harry Bosch novel *Angels Flight* is named for DTLA's historic short railway; the novel was the inspiration for much of season four of the TV series, which had several key scenes shot here.

series to be very L.A.-centric, and Bosch himself to be very L.A.-centric, and it doesn't work if it's not that way. It's actually in my contract." For the first four seasons, Connelly was heavily involved in writing and outlining the episodes, but more recently he's stepped back, which allows more time for writing fiction.

I had to ask about a rumor that he once rented Raymond Chandler's old apartment. He was quick to clarify that it was actually Philip Marlowe's apartment in the film version of *The Long Goodbye*. "Robert Altman's version of *The Long Goodbye* with Elliott Gould led me to Chandler," Connelly said. "Reading Chandler made the lightning strike—I wanted to try to do this. That's why I am who I am. I moved out here and found the building. It's historically protected. I knocked on the manager's door and pointed to the apartment from the movie and asked if it was for rent. He said, 'No. Are you a writer?' Many writers had made this pilgrimage. I gave him my *Los Angeles Times* business card and said, 'If anything ever comes up, I'll rent it.' Many years went by, and in 2001 we moved back to Florida. I was ambivalent about the move—L.A. was my muse, it was feeding me my stories—so the deal was that I got to come back regularly to research and keep connections. Two years after we moved, that manager called the number on my card, and it went to someone at the *Times* who still knew me, who got me a message. I called from Florida and rented it over the phone. I kept it as a place to come back and do research. I had it for about four years. While I was there, a lot of would-be writers knocked on the door and asked to see the place, and I knew why." (BTW, it's the High Tower Apartments, at 2178 High Tower Drive.)

Connelly credited a Richard Price quote for shaping his perspective: "When you circle around a murder long enough, you get to know the city." He continued, "I really believe that, and that's one reason why I write these stories. I'd add, when you circle around the detectives who work that murder beat, you really get to know more about the city. There's an irony about it. This city is defined by two things: the entertainment industry and our crime. It makes it an interesting place to write about."

MUST-READ L.A. CRIME FICTION

Hundreds of outstanding contenders fill L.A. bookstore shelves. This is an excellent beginning.

➤ ANGELS FLIGHT (Harry Bosch series), Michael Connelly (1999) • Really, you can start with any of the twenty-one novels featuring LAPD homicide detective Bosch, but this is a favorite.

➤ THE BIG SLEEP, Raymond Chandler (1939) • It's best if you don't think too much about the complicated plot of this noir classic, which has inspired two movies—just enjoy the ride.

➤ THE BLACK DAHLIA, James Ellroy (1987) • This dark novel based on the murder of Elizabeth Short cemented Ellroy's reputation as a first-rate crime writer.

➤ THE BLACK MARBLE, Joseph Wambaugh (1977) • Former LAPD detective Wambaugh found big success writing novels based on his experiences; this one has dark humor and became a movie in 1980.

➤ DAMAGE CONTROL, Denise Hamilton (2011) • An L.A. novel set in the high-powered world of crisis management, dealing with politics, celebrity, and, of course, murder.

➤ DEAD EXTRA, Sean Carswell (2019) • Straight-up 1940s L.A. noir, dark and sharp, but written with a modern eye regarding the role of the dames, who really knew the score.

➤ DEVIL IN A BLUE DRESS, Walter Mosley (1990) • In which we first meet Easy Rawlins, a post-WWII laborer in Watts who loses his job and finds work as a private eye—and who was so good, he was played by Denzel Washington in the movie.

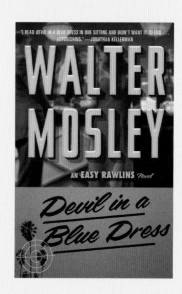

➤ FADEOUT, Joseph Hansen (1970) • Fifty years ago, Hansen broke barriers with this series debut about an openly gay insurance investigator, Dave Brandstetter.

➤ FOLLOW HER HOME, Steph Cha (2013) • Young first-gen Korean American tutor Juniper Song is obsessed with Raymond Chandler and finds herself in the private-eye game.

➤ **GET SHORTY**, Elmore Leonard (1990) • This story following small-time loan shark Chili Palmer is so smart and funny that it inspired both a hit movie and, more recently, a TV series.

➤ **GOOD MAN GONE BAD**, Gar Anthony Haywood (2019) • The latest in the award-winning series following South Central private eye Aaron Gunner.

➤ **GOODNIGHT, IRENE**, Jan Burke (1993) • The debut of a strong series built around journalist-turned-publicist Irene Kelly, who has to rely on her old investigation skills when people start dying.

➤ **HEART ATTACK AND VINE**, Phoef Sutton (2016) • In this second of the Crush novels, Sutton delves into modern-noir territory with a Hollywood story that's funny and fast moving.

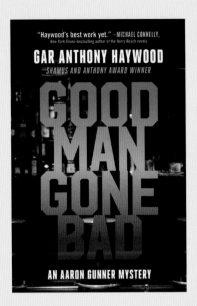

➤ **IN A LONELY PLACE**, Dorothy B. Hughes (1947) • Ask the most writerly of crime writers whom they most admire, and Hughes tops the list; her postwar classic, says noir novelist Megan Abbott, "is a dark, cold gem."

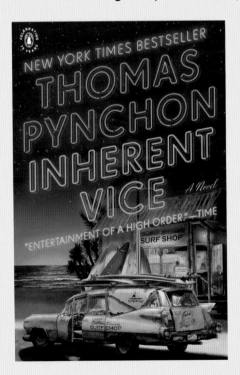

➤ **INHERENT VICE**, Thomas Pynchon (2009) • The surfer-hippie culture of 1970s L.A. comes to life in this darkly funny detective story, which was made into a successful film in 2014.

➤ **INNER CITY BLUES**, Paula L. Woods (1999) • The 1992 L.A. riots provide the backdrop in this series debut as African American LAPD detective Charlotte Justice investigates the murder of a former radical.

➤ **IQ**, Joe Ide (2016) • The first of three rollicking reads starring a solitary genius teenager in East Long Beach.

➤ **KIND OF BLUE**, Miles Corwin (2010) • A former *Los Angeles Times* crime reporter successfully turns his writing talent to the story of a jazz-loving, Jewish LAPD detective.

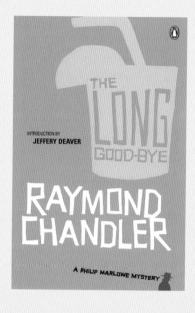

➤ **A KING OF INFINITE SPACE, Tyler Dilts (2010)** • The debut of the Long Beach Homicide series, in which an investigation by homicide detective Danny Beckett opens up old wounds.

➤ **L.A. CONFIDENTIAL, James Ellroy (1990)** • Corruption, sex, and murder intertwine in this hit novel, set in early-1950s L.A.; the film version won a few Oscars.

➤ **L.A. OUTLAWS, T. Jefferson Parker (2008)** • L.A. sheriff Charlie Hood is introduced in this expertly plotted, fast-moving crime thriller.

➤ **LAND OF SHADOWS, Rachel Howzell Hall (2014)** • Hall's deeply engaging protagonist, Elouise Norton, has the nickname "Lockjaw" because of her unwillingness to give up on an investigation, and this debut established her as one of L.A.'s current star fictional detectives.

➤ **THE LONG GOODBYE, Raymond Chandler (1953)** • The sixth Philip Marlowe novel is one of Chandler's best and most personal, written while his wife was dying.

➤ **LOS ANGELES NOIR, edited by Denise Hamilton (2007)** • There are so many good noir short stories that this book got an equally good sequel, but start with this one.

➤ **MILDRED PIERCE, James M. Cain (1941)** • Certainly the greatest Glendale novel of all time, and one of the most beloved in the hard-boiled L.A. canon; read the book first, then watch the Joan Crawford movie.

➤ **THE MOVING TARGET, Ross Macdonald (1949)** • Welcome to Lew Archer, one of L.A.'s most memorable protagonists; he ultimately appeared in eighteen novels—which many consider to be the best detective novels ever written. Fun fact: This series debut features the fictional town of Santa Teresa, which Sue Grafton later used for Kinsey Millhone's hometown.

➤ **THE NEW CENTURIONS, Joseph Wambaugh (1971)** • This groundbreaking cop novel, written by a former LAPD detective, provided an unusually honest look into police life of the era, and remains every bit as compelling today.

➤ **NIGHTTOWN, Timothy Hallinan (2018)** • A laugh-filled story about a burglar-sleuth named Junior Bender who's fast becoming one of L.A.'s favorite fictional felons.

➤ **NO HUMAN INVOLVED, Barbara Seranella (1997)** • Munch Mancini is a fresh L.A. character, an ex-junkie female auto mechanic who flees Venice Beach when she becomes a suspect in the murder of her nasty father.

➤ **THE SONG IS YOU, Megan Abbott (2007)** • Before she turned to psychological thrillers, Abbott did a hell of a job writing super-dark noir, and this one is a standout among standouts, a novel based on the real-life 1949 murder of Jean Spangler.

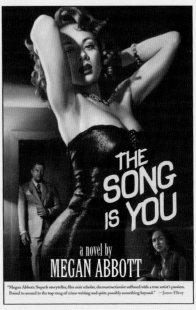

➤ **SOUTHLAND, Nina Revoyr (2003)** • Jumping back and forth from the L.A. of the 1930s, '40s, '60s, and '90s, *Southland* captures parts of the city's life that few writers have ever recorded, with a story that keeps the pages turning.

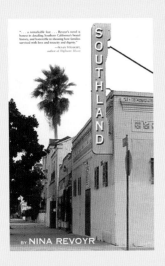

➤ **SUMMER OF THE BIG BACHI, Naomi Hirahara (2004)** • The first of Hirahara's acclaimed Mas Arai series, featuring a doesn't-say-much Japanese American retired gardener from Altadena who stumbles upon more than his fair share of dead bodies.

➤ **THE TWO MINUTE RULE, Robert Crais (2006)** • Crais is rightly praised for his Elvis Cole series, but this standalone thriller about a former bank robber investigating the death of his cop son is a page-turner that careens around L.A.

➤ **VIOLENT SPRING, Gary Phillips (1994)** • Wild, freewheeling L.A. noir, set after the 1992 riots, with African American private eye Ivan Monk searching for the killer of a Korean liquor-store owner.

THE BIG WRITER RAYMOND CHANDLER

RAYMOND CHANDLER'S WORK deserves an entire book devoted to its L.A. literary locations—and, in fact, there have been a couple, both photo-heavy and out of print (*Raymond Chandler's Los Angeles* by Elizabeth Ward and Alain Silver, and *Daylight Noir* by Catherine Corman). To narrow the focus of my search, I decided to look into his Hollywood footprint. The corner of Kenmore and Franklin felt like a good starting place, since Philip Marlowe's apartment was located there in *The Big Sleep*. Marlowe moved around over the course of the novels, but *The Big Sleep* is where he began.

At the corner of Kenmore and Franklin are two apartment complexes and two churches, each of which would have stood during Chandler's time. The apartments are of the classic 1920s–'40s style seen throughout Los Feliz, Hollywood, and Glendale: two-story stucco-and-wood buildings with courtyards and greenery. Either could have been Chandler's inspiration for Marlowe's home.

Much of the action in *The Big Sleep* takes place west of Marlowe's home, in Hollywood proper (and continuing west to Beverly Hills and Malibu). I headed to the heart of Hollywood and its namesake boulevard, taking in the storefronts that line the famous street. Most of the buildings have been there since Chandler's time, some going as far back as the 1910s and '20s.

The Treloar Building was, and is, on Olive Street, near Sixth, on the west side. The sidewalk in front of it had been built of black and white rubber blocks. They were taking them up now to give to the government, and a hatless pale man with a face like a building superintendent was watching the work and looking as if it was breaking his heart.

— Raymond Chandler, *The Lady in the Lake* (1943)

Even though I lived in Hollywood for years, I felt like I didn't belong as I walked on top of the stars set into the terrazzo sidewalks. This is the land of tourists now.

Next stop was Larry Edmunds, the lone remaining bookstore in a neighborhood that used to have several of them, including the great Stanley Rose Book Shop. Specializing in film and theater books and memorabilia, Larry Edmunds has the look and feel of what Chandler described: "A narrowed cluttered little shop stacked with books from floor to ceiling." A block away, at 6715 Hollywood Boulevard, is the circa-1927 Outpost Building, which was most likely the location for Geiger's rare-book store in the novel. Ducking into the lobby takes you right back to the 1930s, from the original lighting to the shoeshine stand.

Were it possible, I would have tried to follow Marlowe as he tails a suspect out of Geiger's and through Hollywood. I've read the description of that walk many times, especially when I lived nearby. But unfortunately, with the building of the Hollywood & Highland monstrosity, the little streets that he described are gone. So instead of tracing Marlowe's ghostly image, I turned toward another Chandler landmark much closer: Musso & Frank Grill, the oldest

Philip Marlowe worked here, on the seventh floor in *The Big Sleep*, but in later books on the sixth floor. Note, however, that there appears to be no seventh floor.

Chandler wrote like a slumming angel and invested the sun-blinded streets of Los Angeles with a romantic presence.

— ROSS MACDONALD,
source unknown

restaurant in Hollywood, almost directly across the street from Larry Edmunds. Since 1919, it's seen many a writer and many a scene set in its booths or at its bar. Marlowe doesn't visit Musso's in *The Big Sleep*, but he does in *The Long Goodbye*, and Chandler himself was a regular. It wouldn't be a visit to Chandler's Hollywood without stopping for a drink in the New Room (dating from 1955).

After I snagged a barstool and a gin martini (the best choice at Musso's), it was time to reflect on Marlowe and the vision of the city his creator gave us. From its earliest days, Los Angeles was marketed as the land of sunshine and fulfilled dreams of prosperity, land ownership, and fame, a place of endless possibility and appeal. For some, those dreams more or less came true. But Chandler saw something dark under the bright California sun. Successful or not, people are still flawed, motivated by big secrets and small lies, jealousy, and pettiness. All of which can lead to darkness and crime. That's been as true for the real Los Angeles as it's been for the fictional one.

There was no murderer to chase during my adventure. No femme (or homme) fatale tried to distract me from my work and lead me astray. True, there was the temptation of more gin, but I resisted. After I finished my martini, the sunshine outside was startling. From there, a walk east on Hollywood Boulevard led to its intersection with Cahuenga Boulevard. It's officially called Raymond Chandler Square because Marlowe's office was in what Chandler called the Cahuenga Building (on the fictional seventh floor in *The Big Sleep* and on the sixth floor in later books). It's actually the 1921 Security Bank Building, which has long been closed for renovations that, at the time of this writing, still haven't happened. It was a strange but sentimental place to end this journey.

MORE CHANDLER LOCATIONS

A few more spots around town that still look as Chandler described:

- **GREYSTONE MANSION** (905 Loma Vista Drive, Beverly Hills), used as the model for General Sternwood's estate in *The Big Sleep*
- **BULLOCKS WILSHIRE** (3050 Wilshire Boulevard, Koreatown), the "green-tinged" art deco masterpiece in *The Big Sleep* that is now Southwestern Law School
- **MALIBU PIER**, where a Buick with a body in it washes up in *The Big Sleep*
- **THE BRYSON APARTMENT HOTEL** (2701 Wilshire Boulevard, Westlake), a Beaux-Arts landmark that appears in *The Lady in the Lake*

MUSSO & FRANK GRILL

Musso & Frank Grill, better known as Musso's, has been a Hollywood staple since 1919. It hasn't changed much since then, with its long-seasoned staff in red-coated livery continuing to deliver flannel cakes, sand dabs meunière, and the best martini in the city (by *GQ*'s reckoning, the best in the country).

Over the past century, Musso's has been a hangout for writers of the page and screen, including those who do both. Such greats of early-twentieth-century American literature as F. Scott Fitzgerald, William Faulkner, John Steinbeck, and Ernest Hemingway found their way to the long-defunct Back Room, which was replaced by the New Room in 1955. Their presence at Musso's paved the way for generations of writers to come, who staked out dark booths or spots at the long bar in the hope that some of the literary genius and Hollywood history would rub off.

Many writers who've frequented Musso's have paid tribute to it in their work. Raymond Chandler sent Philip Marlowe there for dinner in *The Long Goodbye*. Charles Bukowski memorialized it in two novels, *Hollywood* and *Pulp*. Gore Vidal was such a regular that his memorial was held there in 2012. To this day, authors meet at Musso's for drinks with friends, drinks with agents, or drinks alone while they work on their writing or plot their revenge. As long as Musso's survives, that will continue. Pull up a barstool, order a drink, take out a notebook and pen, and watch the world pass by in a fog of gin.

CHANDLER AT WORK

Now the chic Nomad Hotel, this elegant former office building was Raymond Chandler's workplace from the early 1920s until 1932. His career as an executive at the Dabney Oil Syndicate ended when he was fired for, so the story goes, focusing less on work and more on drinking and women other than his wife. If he hadn't been fired, we'd likely never have had *The Big Sleep* and *The Lady in the Lake*.

A big hard-boiled city with no more personality than a paper cup.

— RAYMOND CHANDLER, *The Little Sister* (1949)

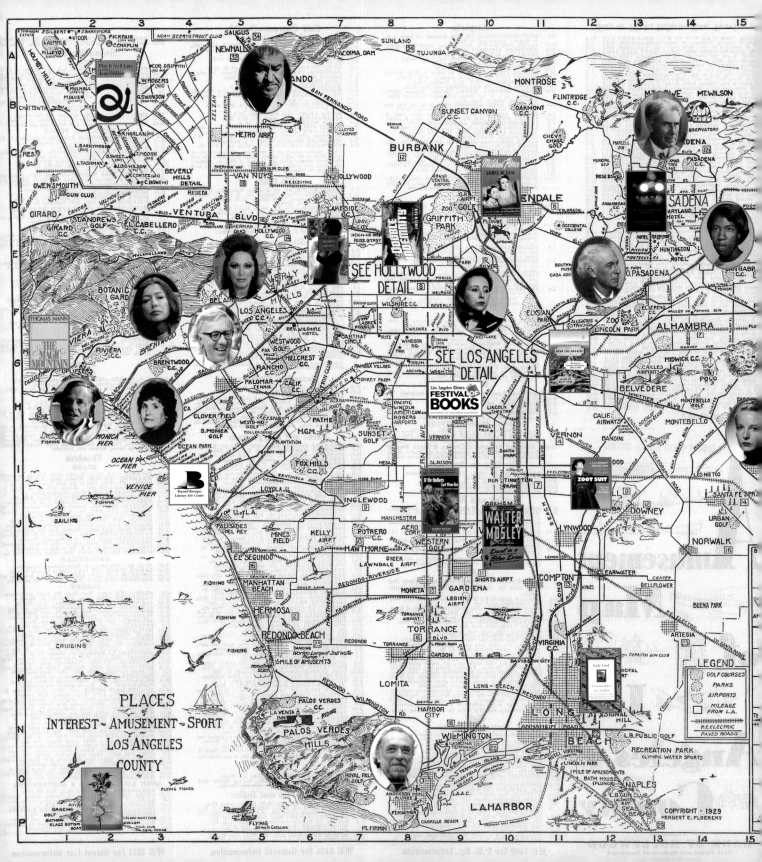

PLACES
of
INTEREST ~ AMUSEMENT ~ SPORT
Los Angeles
COUNTY

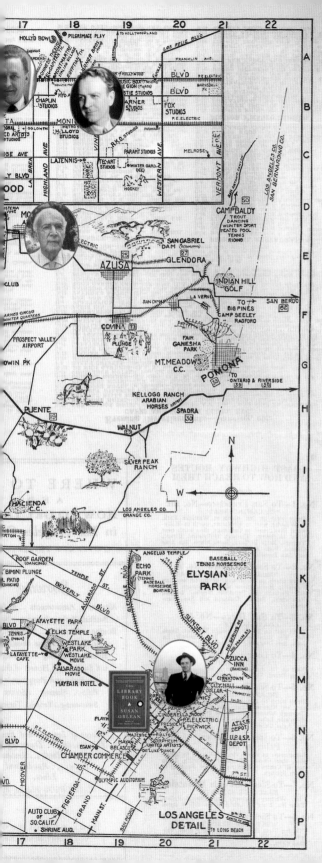

LEGEND

HOLLYWOOD CALLS
AUTHORS ON
STUDIO PAYROLLS

FOR GENERATIONS OF YOUNG creative hopefuls from around the country (and the world), Hollywood has been a draw since the movie industry first blossomed. For a select group of writers during those early years of film, it wasn't just the hope of fame that beckoned, but the power of the movie studios, which brought the most talented among them out to "the Coast" to write for the pictures.

In the 1930s, during the height of the Great Depression, there was money to be made in movies when it wasn't being made anywhere else, and such studio heads as Irving Thalberg ("The Boy Wonder") and Louis B. Mayer called on some of the great American authors of the day to produce scripts. Such literary stars as William Faulkner, Dorothy Parker, and F. Scott Fitzgerald heeded that call and moved west to Los Angeles for the promise of better pay and a reliable gig. It was the studio-system era, when studios had stables of writers, directors, actors, and below-the-line crew who drew steady paychecks and were assigned in-house studio projects, unlike today's gig-economy model, with independent production companies, spec scripts, and freelance work.

While in Los Angeles, Fitzgerald, Parker, and even Ernest Hemingway took up residence in the same hotel on Sunset at Crescent Heights in West Hollywood: the Garden of Allah, named for its original owner, actress Alla Nazimova. Not only did some of the best writers in American letters live in that hub of fame and debauchery, so did actors like Barbara Stanwyck, Greta Garbo, and Errol Flynn, who conducted his many affairs in his Garden of Allah villa.

In her book *The Garden of Allah*, Sheilah Graham, Fitzgerald's assistant turned lover, wrote, "It was a microcosm of its immediate world, a reflection of Hollywood. And what was Hollywood but a city built on a gossamer foundation of fantasy?" Her writing forms a picture of a community gathered loosely around the pool,

> If my books had been any worse, I should not have been invited to Hollywood, and if they had been any better, I should not have come.
>
> — RAYMOND CHANDLER, in a 1945 interview

sharing drinks, gossip, and intrigues. The Garden of Allah functioned as the Algonquin Round Table of the West Coast, with Algonquin regulars Dorothy Parker and Robert Benchley as regular long-term guests.

The writers of that era drank at the same haunts also, often making the short trip east into Hollywood itself to Musso & Frank Grill (see page 20). Musso's claims that Faulkner was so familiar with the bartenders in the Back Room that they let him make his own mint juleps. Musso's long literary-alcohol connection continued with such authors as Charles Bukowski, who regularly drank in the bar in the New Room, which dates to 1955, about as "old" as L.A. gets. Novelists, journalists, and screenwriters today still meet at Musso's for a martini and a menu that's barely changed in a hundred years.

Dorothy Parker, 1935

As much as some of these writers would have liked, their time in Hollywood wasn't all affairs at the Garden of Allah and stiff drinks at Musso's. They also had to produce pages to continue to receive their weekly stipends, which for many were actually pretty modest. The financial challenges for the workaday writer, in fact, inspired Parker to get involved as an organizer wtih the Screenwriters Guild. She wrote:

F. Scott Fitzgerald, 1937

> It is difficult to speak of screen writers. They are not essentially absurd; but such folk as Westbrook Pegler, if I may use the word folk, have set it in the public mind that every writer for the screen receives for his trash $2,500 a week. Well, you see, the average wage of a screen writer is $40 a week, and that for an average of fourteen weeks in the year, and that subject to being fired with no notice.

The writing life, however, was lucrative for some, especially those with name recognition and literary talent. And some were more prolific than others. Parker wrote more than a dozen films with her husband and screenwriting partner, Alan Campbell, including the original *A Star Is Born*, with cowriter Robert Carson, for which they received an Academy Award nomination. Fitzgerald received credit for only one film, *Three Comrades*, in the year and a half that he was under contract at MGM. Faulkner was more productive, receiving credit for six screenplays while at Fox, including adaptations of Raymond Chandler's *The Big Sleep* and Ernest Hemingway's *To Have and Have Not*.

For some of these writers, their time enmeshed in the Hollywood system gave them material for their fiction. Fitzgerald not only wrote *The Pat Hobby Stories* about a screenwriter, but until his death he was working on a novel about a studio head, sometimes called *The Last Tycoon* or *The Love of the Last Tycoon*, depending on which posthumously released incomplete edition one picks up. Faulkner preferred to write about his home state of Mississippi and his fictional Yoknapatawpha County, setting only one short story in Los Angeles, "Golden Land," which is included in David L. Ulin's *Writing Los Angeles*—along with the Faulkner quote:

"I don't like this damn place any better than I ever did."

ESOTOURIC: BOOK TOURING IN L.A.

For more than a dozen years, historians Kim Cooper and Richard Schave have led the city's quirkiest, smartest, and most literary tours and salons, as appealing to lifelong Angelenos as to visitors. Their subjects go beyond books, but it's the bookish ones, of course, that we're here to discuss. The tours vary with the season and year, so you'll have to go to esotouric.com for details. But if you're lucky, you might get to take Los Angeles Book Land, 1939: Chandler, Fante, Huxley, Isherwood, West—a four-hour adventure that celebrates the year that brought readers *The Day of the Locust*, *The Big Sleep*, *Ask the Dust*, and more. Other worthy tours include Birth of Noir: James M. Cain's Southern California Nightmare; The Real Black Dahlia Crime Tour; and Eastside Babylon Crime Tour. Lots of other tours, focusing on architecture, historic preservation, and tawdry tales of true crime, round out the mix. Check it out on esotouric.com.

SLOW DAYS IN HER HOLLYWOOD EVE BABITZ

EVE BABITZ IS A GIFT to readers who want to undertake a literary tour of L.A. She wrote vividly and enthusiastically about the city she so obviously loves. (She hasn't published anything new in years, ever since injuries from a fire sent her into reclusion, but rumor has it that she's still writing.) Her memoirs, essay collections, and fiction are grounded in the streets of Los Angeles, and so I chose a few to visit in search of her L.A. footprints.

I began on Cheremoya, a small strip of street in the lower Hollywood Hills where her family lived in the 1960s when she was a teenager. As I drove down Cheremoya, I saw Craftsman houses, dingbat apartment buildings, and classic bungalow courtyards, all of which stood there in her youth. From there, I took the route that I presume she would have regularly taken as she headed to Hollywood High School. In *Eve's Hollywood*, she described the school as "rounded, voluptuous, palm-treed, and banana-leaved," where "men with convertibles and green eyes cruised by at three to watch the girls.... The girls at our school, and I'm sure the girls who attend Hollywood High to this day, were extraordinarily beautiful."

The school's name evokes glamour, as do most places with the word *Hollywood* in them. So often the reality is disappointing. The campus is fenced off, so I contented myself with walking around the exterior perimeter, looking at the murals that cover so many of the walls. Historic Hollywood figures, from Judy Garland to Bruce Lee, grace one building, while another showcases more contemporary art. The image of Valentino as the Sheik has been repainted and updated since the image that appeared in *Eve's Hollywood*; even as the school has modernized over the decades, it continues to honor its Hollywood history.

It's only fitting that after reading in

> *They're right. Los Angeles isn't a city. It's a gigantic, sprawling, ongoing studio. Everything is off the record. People don't have time to apologize for its not being a city when their civilized friends suspect them of losing track of the point.*
>
> — EVE BABITZ, *Slow Days, Fast Company* (1977)

Eve's Hollywood about the figurative path that Babitz took from Hollywood High to L.A. City College over on Vermont (instead of UCLA, where her friends were going), I saw the names of seniors and their intended colleges displayed on the electronic marquee at the edge of campus. I watched for students who were planning to attend UCLA, which she disdained: "Everyone else went to UCLA from Hollywood High and became 'educators.'"

Taking another page from Babitz's high school years, I went to Canter's Deli, where she would go for bagels: "Sally and I had come to take her to Cantor's [*sic*] for a Sunday lox and cream cheese." It was heading into evening, so a bagel didn't seem right; I ordered a Rueben instead and took in the always-entertaining Canter's scene: old Jews and young musicians, three-generation families and wannabe screenwriters.

Next stop: Chateau Marmont, ground zero for many a writer, musician, and actor and a Babitz hangout that appears often in her writing. I drove north on Fairfax to Sunset and cruised west to the Sunset Strip, where she

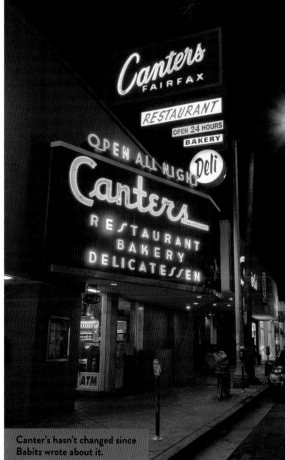

Canter's hasn't changed since Babitz wrote about it.

experienced countless youthful adventures. The Strip is still exciting to me, even though Silver Lake and Echo Park are more of the moment these days. I saw past the current crop of billboards and businesses to imagine the heyday of '70s rock and the men and women who hung out there, buying records at Tower and books at Book Soup by day and playing shows at the Troubadour and the Roxy by night.

At the eastern edge of the Strip is the castle-like Chateau Marmont, which looks exclusive and rather forbidding from the outside. In *Eve's Hollywood*, Babitz wrote, "Ever since the Garden of Allah was torn down and supplanted by a respectable savings and loan institution, the furies and ghosts have made their way across Sunset to the Chateau Marmont." Those furies and ghosts drew me like a moth to the flame, just like they had for Babitz. Let me warn you now: If you want to visit the Marmont, you'll need a few weeks' notice. I discovered the hard way that you can't even get past the valet stand to get a drink without a reservation. They're friendly about their inability to fit you in, but the policy is clear and enforced.

I had to go home and try to get a reservation—no easy feat. I finally returned a few weeks later on a sunny afternoon. It was worth the wait; I understood why she'd spent so much time there. I sipped my frosé, a mix of wine and vodka that I think the young Babitz would have liked (she who chronicled the time she went "over for a drink to a friend's at the Chateau" and didn't leave until two days later), and watched the fashionable people gossip and look fabulous and drop names of productions and projects in development. I also overheard well-heeled tourists making plans for their next stops in L.A.

Hanging out there made me feel far cooler than I usually do, instead of like a nerdy outsider, as I'd expected. I continued to sit there and sip my drink, reading *Slow Days, Fast Company* and

embracing being the sort of woman who thinks nothing of going out for a cocktail alone with a book. I wish I could say I had a Babitz-style encounter with a guy like Jim Morrison or the son of an oil tycoon. But I was totally content having Eve Babitz for company, telling me stories of the Chateau back in the day while I soaked in what it is today. As she wrote in *Black Swans*, "It was the only place in L.A. where, well, *anything* could happen." Sitting there, I sure hoped it would.

The Chateau Marmont today.

SLOW DAYS,
FAST COMPANY
THE WORLD, THE
FLESH, AND L.A.
EVE BABITZ

INTRODUCTION BY
MATTHEW SPECKTOR

Chateau
Marmont
Hotel

CONTEMPORARY L.A. WRITERS TO KNOW

There are thousands, of course, but these are among the city's most talented and prolific. They live everywhere from Montecito to Venice, Manhattan Beach to Indio, and they're all part of the L.A. literary community.

AUTHOR	➤	KNOWN FOR
NOËL ALUMIT	➤	Talking to the Moon
GUSTAVO ARELLANO	➤	Ask a Mexican / Taco USA
EVE BABITZ	➤	Eve's Hollywood / Slow Days, Fast Company / Sex & Rage
AIMEE BENDER	➤	The Particular Sadness of Lemon Cake
TOSH BERMAN	➤	Tosh: Growing Up in Wallace Berman's World
FRANCESCA LIA BLOCK	➤	The Weetzie Bat books
T.C. BOYLE	➤	The Tortilla Curtain / The Harder They Come
MELISSA BRODER	➤	The Pisces / So Sad Today
STEPH CHA	➤	Your House Will Pay
JADE CHANG	➤	The Wangs vs. the World
MARCIA CLARK	➤	Without a Doubt
ROBERT CRAIS	➤	The Two Minute Rule / the Elvis Cole mysteries
NATASHIA DEÓN	➤	Grace
JARED DIAMOND	➤	Guns, Germs, and Steel / Collapse
CATIE DISABATO	➤	The Ghost Network
LIAN DOLAN	➤	Helen of Pasadena / The Sweeney Sisters
TANANARIVE DUE	➤	My Soul to Keep
GEOFF DYER	➤	But Beautiful / Jeff in Venice
HOPE EDELMAN	➤	Motherless Daughters
BRET EASTON ELLIS	➤	Less Than Zero
JAMES ELLROY	➤	L.A. Confidential / The Black Dahlia
STEVE ERICKSON	➤	Zeroville / Shadowbahn
CHRIS ERSKINE	➤	Daditude
PERCIVAL EVERETT	➤	I Am Not Sidney Poitier / Erasure
JANET FITCH	➤	White Oleander / The Revolution of Marina M.
DAVID FRANCIS	➤	Wedding Bush Road
JIM GAVIN	➤	Middle Men
ROXANE GAY	➤	Bad Feminist / Hunger
LYNELL GEORGE	➤	After/Image: Los Angeles Outside the Frame

LEE GOLDBERG	➤	True Fiction / publisher of Brash Books
TOD GOLDBERG	➤	Gangsterland / Other Resort Cities
REYNA GRANDE	➤	The Distance Between Us
RACHEL HOWZELL HALL	➤	The Eloise "Lou" Norton mysteries
TIMOTHY HALLINAN	➤	The Junior Bender mysteries
DENISE HAMILTON	➤	The Jasmine Trade / Los Angeles Noir
NAOMI HIRAHARA	➤	The Mas Arai mysteries / Farewell to Manzanar
MEG HOWREY	➤	The Wanderers
MICHELLE HUNEVEN	➤	Blame / Jamesland / Round Rock
JOE IDE	➤	The IQ mysteries
CHIP JACOBS	➤	Smogville / Arroyo
LISKA JACOBS	➤	Catalina
NOVA JACOBS	➤	The Last Equation of Isaac Severy
DANA JOHNSON	➤	In the Not Quite Dark
JULIA CLAIBORNE JOHNSON	➤	Be Frank with Me
JONATHAN & FAYE KELLERMAN	➤	When the Bough Breaks (him) / Bone Box (her)
DAVID KIPEN	➤	Dear Los Angeles: The City in Diaries and Letters
JIM KRUSOE	➤	Iceland / Girl Factory
LAILA LALAMI	➤	The Moor's Account
EDAN LEPUCKI	➤	California / Woman No. 17
ATTICA LOCKE	➤	Bluebird, Bluebird / Heaven, My Home
LEWIS MacADAMS	➤	Birth of the Cool
SARAH MANGUSO	➤	300 Arguments
STEVE MARTIN	➤	Shopgirl / Born Standing Up
ALISTAIR MCCARTNEY	➤	The End of the World Book / The Disintegrations
MAILE MELOY	➤	Liars and Saints / Do Not Become Alarmed
PATT MORRISON	➤	Don't Stop the Presses
YXTA MAYA MURRAY	➤	Locas
GINA B. NAHAI	➤	Moonlight on the Avenue of Faith / Cry of the Peacock
SONIA NAZARIO	➤	Enrique's Journey
MAGGIE NELSON	➤	Bluets / The Argonauts
VIET THANH NGUYEN	➤	The Sympathizer / The Refugees
B.J. NOVAK	➤	One More Thing
SCOTT O'CONNOR	➤	A Perfect Universe / Half World

SUSAN ORLEAN	➤	The Library Book / The Orchid Thief
WENDY C. ORTIZ	➤	Excavation / Hollywood Notebook
LIZA PALMER	➤	Conversations with the Fat Girl
T. JEFFERSON PARKER	➤	L.A. Outlaws / Laguna Heat
VICTORIA PATTERSON	➤	This Vacant Paradise
THOMAS & JO PERRY	➤	The Old Man (him) / Dead Is Better (her)
GARY PHILLIPS	➤	The Obama Inheritance / Orange County Noir
SALVADOR PLASCENCIA	➤	The People of Paper
IVY POCHODA	➤	Wonder Valley
TAYLOR JENKINS REID	➤	Daisy Jones & the Six
NINA REVOYR	➤	A Student of History / Southland / The Age of Dreaming
LUIS J. RODRIGUEZ	➤	Always Running
STEVEN ROWLEY	➤	Lily and the Octopus
MARK SALZMAN	➤	Lying Awake / Iron & Silk
LISA SEE	➤	On Gold Mountain / Snow Flower and the Secret Fan
DANZY SENNA	➤	Caucasia
MARISA SILVER	➤	Mary Coin / The God of War
MONA SIMPSON	➤	Anywhere but Here
MARK HASKELL SMITH	➤	Baked / Moist
JERRY STAHL	➤	Permanent Midnight / I, Fatty
J. RYAN STRADAL	➤	Kitchens of the Great Midwest / The Lager Queen of Minnesota
SUSAN STRAIGHT	➤	Highwire Moon / In the Company of Women
PHOEF SUTTON	➤	The Crush mysteries / From Away
MICHELLE TEA	➤	Against Memoir
ANDI TERAN	➤	Ana of California
JERVEY TERVALON	➤	Understand This / Monster's Chef
HÉCTOR TOBAR	➤	The Barbarian Nurseries
MICHAEL TOLKIN	➤	The Player / NK3
DAVID TREUER	➤	Rez Life
DAVID L. ULIN	➤	Sidewalking
ABBI WAXMAN	➤	The Bookish Life of Nina Hill
BEN H. WINTERS	➤	Golden State
DON WINSLOW	➤	The Cartel / The Force / The Border
TERRY WOLVERTON	➤	Insurgent Muse

SEX, DRUGS & MOTION PICTURES

JERRY STAHL

THE ALEXANDRIA HOTEL was once a glamorous hangout for the Hollywood elite, but today it's somewhere between the transitional-housing hub it once was and a gentrified hipster spot, like so many of its neighbors in downtown L.A. Some claim that it's haunted by the ghosts of Rudolph Valentino and other former hotel guests; the still-unoccupied Phantom Wing certainly raises questions. Despite the building's complicated past, the renovations that began in 2005 have transformed the graceful ballrooms and retail spaces into locations for filming, weddings, and events, and the ground floor is now home to a number of newish bars. The Wolves, the newest of the bunch, seeks to capture some of that lost glory, and it almost feels like it's been there since the early 1900s.

I'd arranged to meet Jerry Stahl there because his 2004 biographical novel about Fatty Arbuckle, *I, Fatty*, describes Arbuckle visiting a resident of the Alexandria, and the hotel's role in the early days of cinema history made it appropriate.

I asked the former New Yorker why he moved to L.A. "For reasons too bizarre to explain, I'd been in a YMCA in Columbus, Ohio, for three months," Stahl said. "Then I moved to L.A. for a job at *Hustler* magazine. I wanted to get out of New York to get away from drugs, and coming to L.A. worked out beautifully. I was a journalist and had short stories and the Pushcart Prize and all that, but I didn't know how to survive on that. I never anticipated writing screenplays or TV," which is exactly what he ended up doing. He added, "For me, L.A. was the better place to be broke, having been broke on both coasts. Not to brag."

Writing a novel wasn't Stahl's intent—he was originally researching Arbuckle's life for a biography. "Anthony Bourdain was doing this nonfiction book series for Bloomsbury," he said. "He did one on Typhoid Mary, for example, because she turned out to be a chef." Stahl was originally going to write about Griffith J. Griffith, the man who gave L.A. Griffith Park, but then he stumbled

Photo by Meiki Takechi Arquillos

upon stories about Arbuckle and became fascinated. "But what I was writing sounded like a term paper," he said. "Without asking, I decided to turn it into a novel. Boy, were they not thrilled. It worked out, though, and I have Anthony to thank for that." And so, *I, Fatty* was born.

Stahl related to Arbuckle's outsider status: "I admired his suffering. I was fascinated with the fact that he hooked up with Buster Keaton, whose father used him as a prop in their vaudeville shows, while Arbuckle's father abandoned him in a train station. I related to that stuff."

The more Stahl uncovered about Arbuckle, who was at the center of Hollywood first major scandal when he was charged with (and later cleared of) murdering an actress, the more he was drawn in. "I fell in love with the guy," he said. "Doesn't mean he wasn't a prick—who isn't, on some level, on some days?" Stahl was especially inspired by the places that Arbuckle frequented and his explorations of the city, from riding the streetcar out to Glendale to working at the Mack Sennett Studios to socializing at the swankiest joint in town, the Alexandria.

Stahl's own geography has always filtered into his writing. "I believe landscape is a character," he said. "It informs everyone, and you're shaped by it. Like Joan Didion and her freeways."

Stahl is best known for his 1995 memoir, *Permanent Midnight*, which focuses on his life in the '80s and early '90s as an L.A. TV writer and delves into his addictions and the price he was willing to pay to feed them. It was adapted into a movie starring Ben Stiller, who became a lifelong friend. "I never had a steady gig on TV," Stahl said. "I was fired by all the best shows." When he decided to write his memoir, the longtime scriptwriter had to tackle the challenge of prose. "For me, the difference between writing a book and writing a screenplay is, you write a screenplay and it's like there's three people standing behind you smacking the back of your head and screaming as you type. When you write a book, it's pretty much just you screaming at yourself. It's a different kind of scream."

When I asked if he prefers one of the two types of writing, he replied, "I used to pontificate about that, but ultimately it's about your voice on the page. You can't be too precious in screenwriting because someone is going to rip the shit out of it. And it would be hypocritical of me to complain, because I made my living for a long time rewriting other people. It's just a different delivery engine."

Now, he said, his writing focus is on collaboration: "It's less about the medium, really—you just find someone and hang out all day and see if you, fingers crossed, can get paid for it. Being in a writers' room, just working together on something, that's great. Writing books can be a little crazy-making. On a good day, for me, TV and movies are a healthier form of crazy-making."

MUST-READ L.A. NONFICTION

The Southland's libraries and bookstores are packed with enough great L.A.-centric memoirs, anthologies, essay collections, and journalism titles to fill ten books like this. Here are the ones we most adore. (For history books, see page 96; for guidebooks, go to page 106.)

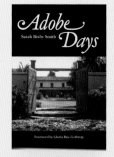

➤ **ADOBE DAYS**, Sarah Bixby Smith (1925) • An engaging memoir of Smith's life as an early Angeleno in the late 1800s and early 1900s.

➤ **AFTER/IMAGE**, Lynell George (2018) • In words and photographs, an L.A. native and accomplished journalist ponders how her city has changed, for worse and better.

➤ **ALL THE SAINTS OF THE CITY OF THE ANGELS**, J. Michael Walker (2008) Art, history, religion, and culture combine in a gorgeous book by a notable L.A. artist.

➤ **ALWAYS RUNNING: LA VIDA LOCA**, Luis J. Rodriguez (1993) • A searing memoir of Rodriguez's days in a Chicano gang in Los Angeles and how he broke free with the help of his poetry, written to inspire the next generation.

➤ **THE ARGONAUTS**, Maggie Nelson (2016) • Part memoir, part theory, this book dives deep into gender identity, love, motherhood, and family. Not for the faint of heart.

➤ **DEAR LOS ANGELES: THE CITY IN DIARIES AND LETTERS 1542–2018**, David Kipen, ed. (2018) • The founder of L.A.'s Libros Schmibros has succeeded in a Herculean task: telling the story of Los Angeles via centuries of fascinating letters and diary entries from the famous, infamous, and unknown.

➤ **GHETTOSIDE: A TRUE STORY OF MURDER IN AMERICA**, Jill Leovy (2015) A *Los Angeles Times* reporter delves into the complexities and tragedies of the plague of murders in low-income, mostly African American communities, using South L.A. as a focal point.

➤ **THE GRIM SLEEPER: THE LOST WOMEN OF SOUTH CENTRAL**, Christine Pelisek (2017) • With passion and anger, an L.A.-based investigative journalist for *People* magazine details the hunt for a serial killer and gives overdue attention to his victims, who were ignored at the time of their deaths.

➤ **HELTER SKELTER, Vicent Bugliosi with Curt Gentry (1974)** • The prosecuting attorney in the Manson murder trial recounts the complexities of this era-defining case; his theories are now doubted by some.

➤ **HOLLYWOOD BABYLON, Kenneth Anger (1965/1975)** • Hollywood scandal stories by the truckload—lots of conjecture and gossip, but a delicious junk-food indulgence regardless.

➤ **HOLLYWOOD NOTEBOOK, Wendy C. Ortiz (2015)** • Ortiz's memoir composed of prose-poem fragments maps Los Angeles as defined by love and loss.

➤ **HOLY LAND: A SUBURBAN MEMOIR, D.J. Waldie (1996)** • A masterful memoir about life in the tract-house L.A. suburb of Lakewood. It became a bestseller for a reason.

➤ **INLANDIA, Gayle Wattawa, ed. (2006)** • L.A.'s all-too-neglected Inland Empire is the focus of this sweeping and impressive anthology that reaches back to the diaries of explorer Juan Bautista de Anza, through memoirs of First Peoples, and to such essayists, poets, novelists, and journalists as Susan Straight, M.F.K. Fisher, Raymond Chandler, Calvin Trillin, and Marisa Silver.

➤ **INSURGENT MUSE, Terry Wolverton (2002)** • Part personal memoir, part history of L.A.'s creatively important Woman's Building, this book adds richness to the city's artistic and literary backstory.

➤ **LETTERS TO MY CITY, Mike Sonksen (2019)** • In poems and essays, this devoted son of Los Angeles (and expert on its literary culture) explores his city.

➤ **LOS ANGELES: PORTRAIT OF A CITY, Jim Heimann (2009)** • A stunning photographic portrayal of L.A. from its earliest days to today, with essays by David L. Ulin and Kevin Starr.

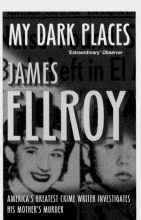

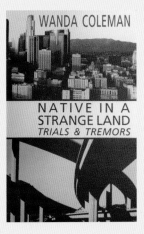

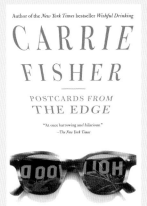

➤ **MY DARK PLACES**, James Ellroy (1996) • This raw, honest autobiography focuses on Ellroy's tortured past and his investigation of the murder that inspired his crime-fiction career: his mother's.

➤ **NATIVE IN A STRANGE LAND: TRIALS & TREMORS**, Wanda Coleman (1996) • This curated selection of Coleman's journalism/personal narrative reveals the heart of Los Angeles, with all of its caricature, glitter, darkness, and transformation.

➤ **PAPERBACK L.A.**, Susan LaTempa, ed. (2018 & 2019) • An engagingly curated three-book series that weaves together essays, fiction, journalism, song lyrics, and quotes from L.A. writers from the nineteenth century to present day, with contemporary photo essays as well.

➤ **PERMANENT MIDNIGHT**, Jerry Stahl (1995) • Stahl's memoir is brutally honest about the price of his heroin addiction and his wild and reckless behavior as a high-rolling, self-loathing Hollywood writer.

➤ **POSTCARDS FROM THE EDGE**, Carrie Fisher (1987) • A rat-a-tat, hilarious memoir about addiction, celebrity, family, and Hollywood.

➤ **SEX, DEATH AND GOD IN L.A.**, David Reid, ed. (1992) • Such respected voices as Eve Babitz, Alexander Cockburn, Mike Davis, Lynell George, Rubén Martínez, and Carolyn See contributed to this engaging collection of essays.

➤ **SIDEWALKING: COMING TO TERMS WITH LOS ANGELES**, David L. Ulin (2015)
Yes, people do walk in L.A., and Ulin does it with thoughtfulness, insight, and engaging prose.

➤ **SLOUCHING TOWARDS BETHLEHEM & THE WHITE ALBUM**, Joan Didion (1968 & 1979) • Iconic, foundational essays that focus on Los Angeles and Southern California, from Manson to Malibu, the Santa Anas to the Sunset Strip.

➤ **SLOW DAYS, FAST COMPANY**, Eve Babitz (1977) • Technically fiction, this is really a memoir of Babitz's freewheeling life in L.A. in the 1970s; as *The New York Times* said, "Babitz writes prose that reads like Nora Ephron by way of Joan Didion, albeit with more lust and drugs and tequila."

➤ **TAKE THIS MAN: A MEMOIR**, Brando Skyhorse (2014) • The true story of a boy's turbulent childhood in Echo Park, growing up with five stepfathers and a mother determined to give her son everything but the truth.

➤ **TATTOOS ON THE HEART**, Gregory Boyle (2010) • The first of two inspirational and sobering memoirs by the founder of Homeboy Industries, who's also a Jesuit priest and L.A. native who has devoted his life to improving the lives of gang members.

➤ **UNDER THE BIG BLACK SUN: A PERSONAL HISTORY OF L.A. PUNK**, John Doe with Tom DeSavia (2016) • The co-founder of X, who turns out to be a fine writer, got a bunch of his punk friends to contribute essays about the powerful L.A. music scene of the late '70s and early '80s.

➤ **WRITING LOS ANGELES: A LITERARY ANTHOLOGY**, David L. Ulin, ed. (2002) • Sprawling and fascinating, this is the essential anthology for anyone trying to understand the shifting, multifaceted L.A. experience.

➤ **A YEAR IN VAN NUYS**, Sandra Tsing Loh (2001) • A hilarious memoir about living the anti-Hollywood L.A. experience.

If, while watching the sun set on a used-car lot in Los Angeles, you are struck by the parallels between this image and the inevitable fate of humanity, do not, under any circumstances, write it down.

— Fran Lebowitz, *The Fran Lebowitz Reader* (1994)

PLAY IT AS SHE DOES

JOAN DIDION

PLAY IT AS IT LAYS, Joan Didion's classic 1970 Los Angeles novel, centers on Maria Wyeth, a minor actress who's lost in the shadow of her movie-director ex-husband and finds herself drifting around L.A. (and getting an abortion) after the institutionalization of her young daughter. It captures the wealth of 1960s Los Angeles, as well as the ennui that plagues Maria.

For many readers of *Play It as It Lays*, the image of Maria driving all day as she seeks form and function in her life is the most enduring, and these scenes are often quoted in pieces about Los Angeles: "Once she was on the freeway and had maneuvered her way to a fast lane, she turned on the radio at high volume and she drove.... She drove it as a riverman runs a river, every day more attuned to its currents, its deceptions, and just as a riverman feels the pull of the rapids in the lull between sleeping and waking, so Maria lay at night in the still of Beverly Hills and saw the great signs soar overhead at seventy miles an hour."

Maria explores more of L.A. than just its freeways. Though much of the city has changed in the decades since Didion wrote the novel, she offers enough sketches of locations to paint a picture of Maria's wealth and to give us a feel for her city.

In pursuit of Maria's L.A., I started in Malibu. Her friends BZ and Helene live "at the beach," and Maria spends time at their home. The exact location of their beachfront house is never divulged, although the Trancas area of Malibu, where Didion and husband, John Gregory Dunne, lived for eight years, is the likely location. While waiting to arrange her abortion, Maria "drove to the beach.... When she got back into town she drove aimlessly down Sunset, pulled into a drive-in at the corner of La Brea," and drank a Coca-Cola. I decided to do the same. After visiting Malibu, I drove back into L.A. along Sunset, thinking about Maria's search for purpose as I wandered like she did.

My first stop as I drove east on Sunset was Beverly Hills, where Maria and her soon-to-be-ex-husband, Carter, live for a time. She spends much of the book by the pool, reading, sleeping, or lying out in the sun. Didion doesn't give them a specific street, so I headed for the heart of town, parking on Rodeo Drive, just south of the Beverly Hills Hotel. I set off for an easy walk down the wide, tree-lined streets, noting that while the houses vary considerably in architectural style, they are uniform in size and isolation. Most have walls, gates, or lavish landscaping separating them from the street and one another. Each house feels cut off from the next, and I got no sense of neighborliness. Didion uses the sequestration of these homes to create an external representation of Maria's distance from everyone else. Maria is isolated throughout *Play It as It Lays*, never connecting with the other characters, and wandering the residential streets of Beverly Hills amplified that feeling of isolation for me. Beautiful and closed off to outsiders, those streets exude an air of loneliness.

I got back into my car and continued east on Sunset to the street where Maria takes an apartment after leaving Beverly Hills. Again, Didion is not specific about the location, but she gives clues: "She had found [the apartment manager] not in the apartment marked 'Mgr.' but out on Fountain Avenue, hosing down the sidewalk." I parked and walked along apartment-lined Fountain in West Hollywood, recognizing some of the prosaic places Didion mentions, like the Ralph's supermarket. It

In the aftermath of the wind the air was dry, burning, so clear that she could see the ploughed furrows of firebreaks on distant mountains. Not even the highest palms moved. The stillness and clarity of the air seemed to rob everything of its perspective, seemed to alter all perception of depth, and Maria drove as carefully as if she were reconnoitering an atmosphere without gravity. Taco Bells jumped out at her. Oil rockers creaked ominously.

— JOAN DIDION, *Play It as It Lays*

was easy to picture Maria holed up in one of the handsome apartments on Fountain, many of which date to the 1920s through the '50s. Unlike the quiet and isolation of Beverly Hills, here the traffic is heavier, and residents share walls.

Maria leaves her Beverly Hills house over a backed-up sink, and she leaves the Fountain Avenue apartment over a backed-up shower, realizing that her problems persist, regardless of where she lives. Carter tells her that the rent on the house is $1,500 a month (more than $9,000 when adjusted for inflation), and he keeps paying the rent after she departs. This reminder fails to motivate her to return to Beverly Hills—Maria's actions are based on emotion, not practicality.

Joan Didion's once-shabby house in the '60s is now a spiritual center.

After visiting Maria's neighborhoods in Beverly Hills and West Hollywood, I returned to Sunset Boulevard and stopped at the corner of La Brea to get a Coke, to echo Maria's journey. From there, it was only a few blocks to the house where Didion famously lived in the late '60s (while she was writing *Play It as It Lays*), at 7406 Franklin Avenue, just west of La Brea (it's now the Shumei spiritual center). Didion describes it in *The White Album*: "Paint peeled inside and out, and pipes broke and window sashes crumbled and the tennis court had not been rolled since 1933, but the rooms were many and high-ceilinged and, during the five years I lived there, even the rather sinistral inertia of the neighborhood tended to suggest that I live in the house indefinitely." She had to leave the rental house in 1971 because its owner planned to tear it down to build a high-rise—but, as with her literature, it still stands today, timelessly elegant.

THE WOMAN'S BUILDING

The genesis of L.A.'s Woman's Building took place in 1973, when artist Judy Chicago, graphic designer Sheila Levrant de Bretteville, and art historian Arlene Raven quit their teaching jobs at CalArts, fed up with what they considered to be an unresponsive, male-dominated culture, and created the Feminist Studio Workshop. They started leading workshops in de Bretteville's house, moving to MacArthur Park in 1973, then moving once again to settle more permanently in a former Standard Oil building in DTLA in 1975; the latter two locations were dubbed the Woman's Building.

At first the focus was on the visual and performing arts, but over time the Woman's Building became a home for such literary tenants as the Sisterhood Bookstore and the Associated Women's Press, and readings and workshops were common. Writers like Audre Lorde and Adrienne Rich spoke there, sharing with other women their commitments to issues ranging from queer rights to feminism to motherhood. Writers who appeared at, taught at, or supported the Woman's Building include Wanda Coleman, Margaret Atwood, and Kate Braverman.

The demand for the workshops and programs eventually diminished, and the Feminist Studio Workshop shut down in 1981. Writer and artist Terry Wolverton, art librarian Sue Maberry, and performance artist Cheri Gaulke took over leadership of the Woman's Building, offering a variety of services to women, from screen printing to writing workshops, before it closed in 1991.

In the intervening years, a few people have brought back some of the education and community of the Woman's Building, including Wolverton, who founded Writers at Work, which provides classes and workshops for writers of all stripes. The Getty Research Institute holds some of the Woman's Building archives and has received a grant to make the collections accessible for future researchers.

Courtesy of the Woman's Building Image Archive at Otis College of Art and Design

HEAVY WOMAN EXPLORATIONS WANDA COLEMAN

FOLLOWING IN THE STEPS of many poets, who lean more abstract and internal than most prose writers, would seem difficult. Fortunately, Wanda Coleman, often called "the unofficial poet laureate of L.A." until her death in 2013, grounded her work in the locations of her life, making reference to bus lines and streets and cafés, and I've greatly enjoyed tracing her trajectory through her poems, short stories, journalism, and essays.

Taking a cue from her poem "Hecuba on Sunset," in which the narrator rides the bus east on Sunset out of Hollywood, beginning at Gower, I followed the bus route in my car. I could picture the characters her narrator sees along Sunset. Other than the Starbucks in the old Gower Gulch corner strip mall, the intersection of Sunset and Gower looks much like it did in the 1980s, when *Heavy Daughter Blues*, the collection in which the poem appears, was published. At Vermont, I took Coleman's instructions on how to drive to Watts:

> cruising Hollywood to Watts take Virgil to Beverly down Commonwealth to Wilshire to Hoover south to 23rd to Figueroa south to 54th east to Avalon south to 103rd—30 minutes as the soul flies

can't let go of it. to live is to drive. to have it function

smooth, flawless. to rise with morning and have it start

i pray to the mechanic for heat again and air conditioning

when i meet people i used to know i'm glad to see them until

i remember what i'm driving and am afraid they'll go outside and

see me climb into that struggle buggy and laugh deep long loud

— WANDA COLEMAN, from
"I Live for My Car," in *Imagoes* (1983)

My drive in twenty-first-century traffic lasted longer than thirty minutes, but only a little longer. The route removed me from the familiar, and I found myself trying to analyze what I was seeing while also being an attentive driver in L.A.'s winter rain. Virgil Village is part of my daily commute, and I'm used to the juxtaposition between restaurants like Sqirl and the pupuseria a few blocks north. But the area south of Beverly has less evidence of gentrification, and Virgil is lined with unfussy businesses—auto repair shops, liquor stores, dollar stores—displaying signage indicating that they've been there for decades.

The route traces a path past USC and Exposition Park, and no matter how often I drive it, it always feels like a surprise to go from the Victorian houses to the large campus and imposing museum buildings and new soccer stadium for the Los Angeles Football Club. Around the busy campus is, of course, traffic—lots of it. As Coleman wrote in a love letter to Los Angeles in *Native in a Strange Land*, "You are one long relentless drive nowhere sometimes in circles always in heavy traffic."

The route enters Watts along 103rd Street. I stopped at the train tracks to let two Blue Line trains pass and wondered how this newer public transit system had changed life in Watts since Coleman's younger days. She wrote often in poems and essays of taking the bus. It was an indicator of class and a reminder of the reality that many Angelenos continue to face: being unable to afford to buy and maintain a car. Her later works make more

Watts Coffee House.

references to driving, because by then she was able—barely—to buy a car of her own, famously described in her poem "I Live for My Car."

In the poem "Poetry Lesson Number One," Coleman writes about a gathering of poets in a Watts café "on a diagonal north of the work-shop off 103rd." She was writing about the late Watts Writers Work-shop and the Watts Happening Coffee House, which closed many years ago but was replaced with the Watts Coffee House. So my end point of this journey was breakfast there.

I hoped there'd be a table of poets discussing their work, like the men did in "Poetry Lesson Number One." Instead, the place was filled with families, including a large group celebrating a birthday. Based on the familiar way the patrons and staff talked to one another, it was clearly a community hub. I knew I was an interloper, but they welcomed me anyway, and I was happy to eat my grits and eggs in a place that was meaningful to Coleman. I wished she was still among us, so I could have sat across from her and asked about the challenges of making art in Watts and of being so often unrecognized despite her immense talent.

Fortunately, the National Book Award finalist left behind reams of writing, some of which address those challenges, and Black Spar-row Press has done an excellent job of publishing her works. Unfortunately, however, in 2002 (and for some time after that) Coleman was shunned by many in L.A.'s literary community for writing a negative review in the *Los Angeles Times* of Maya Angelou's memoir *A Song Flung Up to Heaven*. She criticized the book and urged Angelou to dig deeper and do the work Coleman knew she could do. The back-lash led to booksellers removing Coleman's books from their shelves and event organizers excluding her from events. Even today, some aftereffects linger, although they are dissipating, and my hope is that more new readers get to know one of the great poets of Los Angeles, Wanda Coleman.

In order to get the worst possible first impression of Los Angeles one should arrive there by bus, preferably in summer and on a Saturday night.

— CHRISTOPHER ISHERWOOD, *Horizon* magazine

Art Deco palm trees sway their hula skirts
in perfect unison
against a backdrop of gorgeous blue,

and for you I would try it,
though I have always forbidden myself to write
poems about the beach at sunset.

All the clichés for it sputter
like the first generation of neon,
and what attracts me anyway

— ELOISE KLEIN HEALY,
"The Beach at Sunset," from *Passing* (2002)

A FEW GREAT POETS

The City of Angels is thick with poets; always has been, always will be, or so we hope. This list represents just a taste of some all-time greats. Follow Mike "Mike the Poet" Sonksen (aliveinlosangeles.com) to stay connected to the poetry world, and read more about him on page 110.

NAME	➤	KNOWN FOR
REYNA BIDDY	➤	I Love My Love
LAUREL ANN BOGEN	➤	Psychosis in the Produce Department
CHARLES BUKOWSKI	➤	The Pleasures of the Damned: Poems 1951–1993
VICTORIA CHANG	➤	Barbie Chang
WANDA COLEMAN	➤	Bathwater Wine
BRENDAN CONSTANTINE	➤	Calamity Joe
KAMAU DAÁOOD	➤	The Language of Saxophones
KIM DOWER	➤	Sunbathing on Tyrone Power's Grave
STEPHANIE FORD	➤	All Pilgrim
SESSHU FOSTER	➤	City of the Future / World Ball Notebook
AMY GERSTLER	➤	Scattered at Sea
DANA GIOIA	➤	Pity the Beautiful
ELOISE KLEIN HEALY	➤	Artemis in Echo Park / Passing
JUAN FELIPE HERRERA	➤	Love after the Riots
DOUGLAS KEARNEY	➤	The Black Automaton
ROBIN COSTE LEWIS	➤	Voyage of the Sable Venus
SUZANNE LUMMIS	➤	Open 24 Hours / Editor of Wide Awake
LEWIS MacADAMS	➤	Dear Oxygen
THOMAS MCGRATH	➤	Letter to an Imaginary Friend
FRED MOTEN	➤	The Feel Trio
CAROL MUSKE-DUKES	➤	Sparrow
MAGGIE NELSON	➤	Jane: A Murder
MORGAN PARKER	➤	There Are More Beautiful Things Than Beyoncé / Magical Negro
LUIS J. RODRIGUEZ	➤	The Concrete River
YESIKA SALGADO	➤	Corazón
MIKE SONKSEN	➤	Letters to My City
AMY UYEMATSU	➤	30 Miles from J-Town

DUNBAR HOTEL

If you were a jazz fan in the 1930s and '40s, you would have moved heaven and earth to get to the chic Dunbar Hotel. It was the heart of Central Avenue's swinging jazz era, and where Count Basie, Lena Horne, Duke Ellington, Billie Holiday, and Josephine Baker all performed. From Thurgood Marshall to W.E.B. Du Bois, the Who's Who of America's black elite, including many writers, stayed there regularly; Langston Hughes lived there for a time. In fact, the hotel was named for an author: African American poet and fiction writer Paul Laurence Dunbar. Dentist John Somerville, the first black graduate of USC, built the hotel in 1928 and called it Hotel Somerville, but lost it shortly thereafter in the stock market crash. Its new white owners recognized the hotel's artistic and cultural significance and renamed it in honor of Dunbar, then sold it a year later to an African American businessman, who opened a cabaret and put the Dunbar on the national map.

Eventually the end of forced segregation meant that black stars started staying at places like the Beverly Hills Hotel, and the Dunbar fell on hard times. More recently, however, it was handsomely restored and turned into a center for affordable housing for seniors and families, with more upscale apartments, a café, and event spaces in the surrounding complex.

ALWAYS RUNNING THROUGH L.A. LUIS J. RODRIGUEZ

LUIS J. RODRIGUEZ FOUNDED Tía Chucha Press when he lived in Chicago, but upon moving back to Los Angeles, he expanded its mission and created a bookstore and cultural center as well, all located together in Sylmar. Tía Chucha is at the heart of his work, so it was the perfect place to meet to discuss not only his best-known book, *Always Running*, but also his time as poet laureate of Los Angeles and his continued commitment to sharing both his stories and those of writers he admires.

While a staff of volunteers bustled around us, our conversation began with Tía Chucha itself and Rodriguez's reasons for creating the space. It's a cheerful place, a large room divided into three areas: shelves of books from the press and by Rodriguez; a meeting and performing space with tables and vivid murals; and an altar devoted to Rodriguez's aunt, his Tía Chucha, for whom the center is named. In 2000, after years in Chicago as a journalist, poet, and small-press publisher, he and his family relocated to L.A. They settled in Sylmar to be close to his wife Trini's family, rather than return to the south San Gabriel Valley of his youth, where he had gotten involved with a gang, became a drug user, and been arrested more than once. His teenage son had been getting into trouble of his own, and Rodriguez wanted him in a different environment.

The northeast San Fernando Valley, however, was not without serious challenges. "There was a gap in the community—there was no cultural center," he said. "Half a million people live in the northeast Valley, eighty percent of whom are Mexican and Central American. These are working-class people, and a lot of jobs had gone and many of them were left hanging." His wife had grown up in nearby Pacoima, which, he said, "has a forty-seven percent unemployment rate, one of the elementary schools has twenty-five percent homeless students, and there are housing projects. It has a lot of inner-city problems, but no one thinks of the Valley that way." He and Trini wanted

Luis and Trini Rodriguez.

to help make the region a better place. "We opened the only bookstore here, the only cultural space, the only movie house and art gallery. We had just come from Chicago, where there was so much cultural vibrancy, and we decided to bring some of that, along with some of the '60s/'70s Chicano civil-rights-movement spirit, and have it all come together at Tía Chucha's."

He said, "I'm glad I'm here, especially with Tía Chucha's and what we're doing. I'm a south San Gabriel and East L.A. guy, but I've been in Sylmar nineteen years, so now I'm a Valley guy."

LOVE POEM TO LOS ANGELES
(AN EXCERPT)
Luis J. Rodriguez

The city beckoned as I tried to escape
the prison-like grip of its shallowness,
sun-soaked image, suburban quiet,
all disarming,
hiding the murderous heart
that can beat at its center.
L.A. is also lovers' embraces,
the most magnificent lies,
the largest commercial ports,
graveyard shifts,
poetry readings,
murals,
lowriding culture,
skateboarding,
a sound that hybridized
black, Mexican, as well as Asian
and white migrant cultures.

Excerpted from "Love Poem to Los Angeles," published in *Borrowed Bones* (2016, Curbstone Books/Northwestern University Press).

In *Always Running*, Rodriguez writes about dropping out of Cal State L.A.'s journalism program and turning to manual labor and factory/industrial work. But words still mattered—a lot. "I don't think the writing calling ever left me," he said. "I had started writing when I was young, in jail and juvenile hall, and I didn't know what I was doing. Some of what I did got attention, and I got honorable mention in a literary contest when I was eighteen. But to avoid jail and gangs and drugs, I worked in industrial jobs. That's demanding; sometimes I was working sixteen-hour days. You can't write in those conditions, but I always had that bug and couldn't let it go."

When he and his first wife divorced, he said, he saw that as his chance to do what he wanted to do. "By the 1980s, I made the big move and quit all my industrial jobs and started working for weekly newspapers in East L.A.," he said. *It Calls You Back*, his second memoir volume, gets into the challenges of that time for him: "There was a lot more struggle, and *It Calls You Back* means the madness will keep calling you back. I wasn't going to go back to gangs, crime, and drugs anymore, but I was called by rage and alcoholism and bad relationships."

Rodriguez actually liked the work in construction and factories, but he realized that he loved to write more. "When I made the decision to work in journalism, that gave me time to write," he said. While working for newspapers or news radio, he'd write his own stuff on the side, and years later, when *Always Running* became a big hit, he quit the day jobs.

His own writing and the history of his press have often intertwined. "I published my first book through what became Tía Chucha Press," he said. "I didn't know it was going to become a press. A friend designed that first book, and it was so beautiful that all these Chicago poets asked if I could produce their books, and that's how it started. That same designer has been working with me for thirty years now."

Rodriguez's second book, *The Concrete River*, was picked up by Curbstone Press in Connecticut, and it sold thousands of copies. "That just doesn't happen in poetry," he said. "*Concrete River* opened up a whole literary world for me. I was amazed that people were paying attention to my work."

Later came the runaway success of *Always Running*. "The idea came to me because my son was in trouble with gangs," he said. "I had twenty years' worth of writing about my experiences, and I decided to put it together into a book." He wrote it as a novel, but his editor at Curbstone thought it wasn't quite working, so he reshaped it into a memoir, and it came out as a hardcover. "The L.A. uprising had happened the year before, so

Twelve cars full of armed homies caravanned north on the 605 through Downey, Montebello, Temple City, and into Arcadia, the city's hood like any other. Manzo wondered if there was a big factory somewhere that manufactured fucked-up apartment buildings, raggedy houses, liquor stores, and strip malls just for poor people.

— Joe Ide, *Righteous* (2017)

everybody wanted to know about L.A. gangs," he said. "I was on *Oprah*, *Good Morning America*, and *Fresh Air*. I traveled to thirty cities in three months. The book did so well that all these New York big-time publishers were vying for the paperback rights. It was a once-in-a-lifetime thing. I've written fifteen books and have never been able to replicate that."

In the wake of *Always Running*'s success, Rodriguez became an in-demand speaker and respected author. "I love talking to people," he said. "Especially young people. It's the best thing going." And he was chosen as L.A.'s poet laureate, a post he held from 2014 to 2016. "That was a popular thing," he said. "I was not anticipating that. I got to speak at hundreds of venues. They wanted me to do a minimum of six events a year; I did 110 the first year. The next year I did even more. I did it because it was such a rare opportunity to speak to people about poetry."

What's next? "Poetry is my favorite, but lately I've been writing a lot of essays and op-eds," he said. "Next, I'll have a book of essays coming out. I've also got a podcast with my wife, and I'm working on a YouTube channel.

"I just want to speak to America as much as I can."

It never stopped, this running. We were constant prey, and the hunters soon became big blurs: the police, the gangs, the junkies, the dudes on Garvey Boulevard who took our money, all smudged into one. Sometimes they were teachers who jumped on us Mexicans as if we were born with a hideous stain. We were always afraid. Always running.

— Luis J. Rodriguez, *Always Running* (1993)

L.A. PUBLISHERS

It's unlikely that anyone who works in publishing in New York will believe that L.A. is home to more than three dozen publishers, but it is. There are more than what's listed here—we did our best to find the most notable ones.

➤ **THE ACCOMPLICES** • Three L.A. nonprofits—Writ Large Press, Civil Coping Mechanisms (a book publisher), and Entropy (a literary journal)—have joined forces and are publishing marginalized voices, especially writers of color.

➤ **ANGEL CITY PRESS** • L.A. treasures Paddy Calistro and Scott McAuley have been publishing gorgeous illustrated books about Southern California history and culture for more than twenty-five years.

➤ **ASYLUM PRESS** • Comics and graphic novels, with specialties in horror and comedic adventure.

➤ **BABY TATTOO** • Beloved at Comic-Con and by Gris Grimly and Brian Kesinger fans, Baby Tattoo publishes visually stunning books that defy categorization.

➤ **BALCONY PRESS** • Design-intensive trade and custom books, with a focus on architecture, design, and photography.

➤ **BRASH BOOKS** • Bestselling writer Lee Goldberg and partner Joel Goldman publish crime, suspense, and thriller fiction, with a particular passion for bringing back worthy crime fiction that has fallen out of print.

➤ **BROWN PAPER PRESS** • Based in Long Beach, Wendy Thomas Russell's press produces a mix of prescriptive nonfiction and engaging memoir.

➤ **CHRONICLE CHROMA** • Founded by the folks behind AMMO, this new Chronicle imprint is focusing on visual arts and pop culture with an L.A. vibe.

➤ **COUNTERPOINT** • This publisher of smart, often award-winning fiction, memoir, and nonfiction is based in Berkeley, but star editor Dan Smetanka and his small team are in L.A.

➤ **DISNEY PUBLISHING WORLDWIDE** • It's not actively part of L.A.'s book culture, so few people know that there's a large children's book publisher in Glendale, but there is.

➤ **DOPPELHOUSE PRESS** • Carrie Paterson's elegant small press focuses on architecture, design, and art, often involving stories of migration and diaspora.

➤ **GETTY PUBLICATIONS** • Books that complement the Getty's collections, including on art, archaeology, photography, and conversation; it's the kind of house where even the editorial assistants might have PhDs.

➤ **GOLD LINE PRESS & RICOCHET** • Publishing chapbooks and works that jump genres, these tiny sibling presses are run by USC's PhD Program in Creative Writing.

➤ **GREEN INTEGER** • Small-format books, both new and resuscitated classics, that include "essays, manifestos, maxims, epistles, poems, ramblings, revelations" and more.

➤ **HARVARD SQUARE EDITIONS** • Formed by Harvard alumni and once part of Harvard Writers and Publishers, this Hollywood press publishes "literary fiction of social and environmental value."

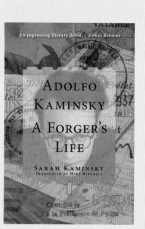

➤ **HAT & BEARD PRESS** • Known for its limited editions, Hat & Beard focuses on illustrated, design-savvy books on art, music, and pop culture.

➤ **HEX COMIX** • Crowdfunded comics with a female focus.

➤ **THE ICE PLANT** • Established by a Macmillan sales rep, this small shop turns out high-end, limited-edition art books that are works of art themselves.

➤ **INSERT BLANC PRESS** • With a dozen projects a year ranging from chapbooks to high-end art books, Insert Blanc also runs the literary podcast *The People*.

➤ **INTERLUDE PRESS** • LGBTQ fiction and romantic fiction, with a newer imprint focusing on YA work.

➤ **INVENTORY PRESS** • A small Silver Lake shop turning out beautifully designed titles on architecture, art, design, and music.

➤ **JADED IBIS PRESS** • A feminist press publishing historically silenced and culturally marginalized voices.

➤ **KAYA PRESS** • Under the auspices of USC, Kaya publishes books of the Asian Pacific diaspora.

➤ **KNOCK KNOCK** • High on design and wit, Jen Bilik's Knock Knock produces gift and humor books, as well as stationery and other paper products.

➤ **LARB BOOKS** • This new nonprofit is an offshoot of the *L.A. Review of Books*, specializing in three areas: classic SoCal books that have fallen out of print, novella-length creative nonfiction, and "philosophical approaches to the contemporary intellectual condition."

➤ **LIL' LIBROS** • A homegrown success created by Patty Rodriguez and Ariana Stein, two young moms who couldn't find quality Spanish-English board books—and now they're publishing the best ones in the country.

➤ **LOS NIETOS PRESS** • Poetry and short fiction from L.A. authors, with a focus on working-class communities.

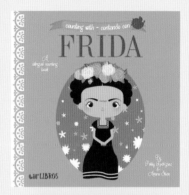

➤ **NOT A CULT** • A relatively new small press publishing poetry, fiction, art titles, and creative nonfiction.

➤ **NOUVELLA BOOKS** • Dedicated to novellas, Nouvella uses a creative form of crowdfunding to finance its books.

➤ **OTIS BOOKS** • A small nonprofit that's part of the MFA program at Otis College of Art and Design, run with student involvement.

➤ **PENNY-ANTE** • An edgy, risk-taking micro-press that focuses on poetry and works that don't fit into genres.

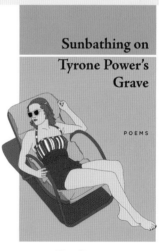

➤ **PROSPECT PARK BOOKS** • Colleen Dunn Bates's Altadena press releases a dozen broadly diverse titles a year: mysteries, cookbooks, humor, fiction, and regional nonfiction—like the book you're reading right now.

➤ **RARE BIRD** • Tyson Cornell took his Book Soup experience and his background as a musician to create L.A.'s largest indie press, publishing everything from musician memoirs to crime fiction to a novel by Sean Penn.

➤ **RED HEN PRESS** • This vibrant Pasadena nonprofit has been publishing respected poetry and literature for more than twenty-five years.

➤ **SAGE PUBLISHING** • Part of an international publishing corporation, this large Thousand Oaks operation produces books for academic and professional markets.

➤ **TASCHEN** • High-production-value books on art, food, culture, design, and cities are the specialties of this German publisher, whose American HQ is in Hollywood.

- ➤ **TÍA CHUCHA PRESS** • Founded by acclaimed poet/essayist Luis J. Rodriguez and his wife, Trini, this is a cultural center as well as a small press that focuses on works from oft-marginalized writers.

- ➤ **TIMBUKTU LABS/REBEL GIRLS** • A new high-profile, female-focused house that started with a bestselling bang: the Rebel Girls books for kids.

- ➤ **TSEHAI PUBLISHERS & HARRIET TUBMAN PRESS** • The mission of these sibling houses, based at Loyola Marymount, is to produce books, conferences, and films "to reverse the gentrification of stories and Africa's brain drain."

- ➤ **UNDERGROUND VOICES** • What started as an online literary magazine has become a literary house that releases several novels and/or novellas a year.

- ➤ **UNNAMED PRESS** • Based in Eagle Rock, this general-trade house publishes about ten titles a year, focusing on first-rate fiction, literature in translation, and memoir.

- ➤ **WORLD STAGE PRESS** • With roots going back to the Watts Writers Workshop, World Stage publishes African American literature.

- ➤ **WRITE BLOODY PUBLISHING** • A poetry house created by poet and former paratrooper Derrick C. Brown.

- ➤ **X ARTISTS' BOOKS** • A new and wildly creative art-focused press established by three L.A. artists, including actor/author Keanu Reeves.

LAX is our failed welcome mat and proof that we don't really care about what outsiders think.

— CHRIS ERSKINE, *Daditude* (2018)

SIDEWALKING TOGETHER
DAVID L. ULIN

DAVID L. ULIN'S *SIDEWALKING* is a meditation on Los Angeles as a psychic space, a space in which the layers of history and the real and imagined city come together. He regularly writes about the Mid-Wilshire neighborhood where he lives and walks, as well as other neighborhoods he visits. *Sidewalking* gives vibrant life to his streets.

One of the touchstones of his walks around LACMA is a piece of programmatic architecture on Wilshire Boulevard. Originally a camera shop called the Dark Room, the storefront still has a giant camera as its façade. Over the years it's been home to a few other businesses, including an Indian restaurant that he frequented. Now it's a bar and restaurant called the Spare Tire, and that's where we met to discuss his work and his city.

Ulin moved to L.A. from New York, "not kicking and screaming, but kind of ambivalently." He agreed to move to support his wife, Rae Dubow, an actress whose opportunities in New York were limited. His connection to his new city's literary scene helped ease the transition. "I don't know if I would have come here if I didn't have a group of friends here already," he said. "A lot of them were writers—screenwriters, novelists, poets, and journalists—and that's how I got connected to the literary community."

These friendships grew out of earlier visits. A friend from college had moved to L.A. and was working at Book Soup and as the books editor at the *Los Angeles Reader*. When Ulin visited from New York, his friend would give him writing assignments and take him to places like Beyond Baroque and Gorky's. Those experiences provided introductions, but they were just a start. "I admired a lot of writers but didn't know them that well," Ulin said. "When we moved here, it became much more important to me. I couldn't figure out a way to get under the surface of the city, so I started attending readings at Beyond Baroque and looking at the poetry magazines. PEN was really important to me. That opened up a portal." As he got to know the

Photo by Noah Ulin

local literary culture, he discovered how different it was from New York's. "What was interesting to me was that writers overlapped," he said. "Not only were we all hanging out together, but everyone was doing more than one thing. I was doing more than one thing, too. It made much more sense to me as a way to work."

That change of pace gave Ulin a new sense of freedom in his writing. "I was hyperaware of the pressure of being a writer living in New York," he said, "and there was something really freeing about coming to a place where someone's reaction to finishing a novel was, 'Why?' I didn't have to worry about what anyone else thought. Nobody was paying much attention, and that was profoundly liberating."

The Guggenheim fellow has been prolific in several fields: journalism, essays, literary history, fiction, and criticism. (Among his many achievements, he was the book critic for the *Los Angeles Times* for several years.) In the early 1990s, he cowrote (with Paul Kolsby) a serial story for the *Los Angeles Reader*, which later became the novel *Ear to the Ground*, published by L.A.'s Unnamed Press. The process of writing that serial also changed his attitude about writing. "Before that, fiction writing felt more fraught. Nonfiction was related to journalism, with deadlines. With fiction I could be such a perfectionist that I'd never finish. But with the serial, we were publishing on Thursday, so your chapter had to be turned in on Tuesday. It was really liberating—I had to get out of my own way to make the deadline."

Ulin also pursued writing nonfiction instead of screenplays: "It was a smaller and more supportive literary community, which I think it still is. I like pushing against the grain a little bit by not pursuing screenwriting, and I like flying under the radar. Also, I'd become really fascinated with the city. It's a really interesting landscape to explore the questions of space and the construction of space."

Sidewalking is one of nine books Ulin has written or edited, so

Visitors to Los Angeles, then and now, were put out because the residents of Los Angeles had the inhospitable idea of building a city comfortable to live in, rather than a monument to astonish the eye of jaded travelers.

— JESSAMYN WEST, *Hide and Seek* (1973)

it's not the first time he's examined the unique spaces of a city. But L.A. carried a different kind of inspiration. "When I was in New York," he said, "I wrote about that city and my relationship to it, a relationship that was inherited from several generations of family. Los Angeles felt like uncharted territory, at least where I was coming from. I realized later that wasn't exactly true, but approaching it from a literary point of view, it felt like wide-open territory."

Ulin often writes about the changeable nature of the city, and he talked about the former camera-shop space in which we sat and how it represents so much of what he writes about in *Sidewalking*. "I'm fascinated by how physical spaces don't change, but their emotional resonance changes depending on future generations that use them," he said. "That's part of the fabric of the emotional density that a city has. Partly because I'm not from here and partly because I'd bought into the East Coast stereotypes, I wasn't aware of the emotional depth that exists here. Looking back at it, I'm aware of all of these elements conspiring together to create this worldview."

Los Angeles has influenced more than Ulin's approach to literary community and writing. "I think of L.A. as the great flattener, the great horizontal landscape," he said. "When I moved to Los Angeles, which is flat and sprawling, I didn't understand it physically, and I didn't understand it emotionally and psychologically. I had to be conscious and understanding; I couldn't take anything for granted. There was a kind of fluidity and mobility that I didn't feel in other places I'd lived, a sense of possibility. In Los Angeles, I found I could be myself in a way I didn't feel I could be in New York."

The most evocative features of Los Angeles can't always be put into words. Sense of place is a connection that takes root. It flourishes deep inside. That spirit of place may come in a quick glimpse or along a periphery. Maybe it's a mood. A hidden vista. The scale of a street. The bend of a skyscraping fan palm. Maybe it's the sound of the wind.

— Lynell George, *After/Image* (2018)

BEYOND BAROQUE

On Venice Boulevard, between Lincoln and Abbot Kinney, sits an old Venice city hall turned literary arts center that draws poetry lovers from across the Southland. Beyond Baroque has hosted literary events here since 1968, providing a salon culture for readers and writers to find one another and discover new work. Readings and workshops are held regularly, and the bookstore and art gallery are open Friday and Saturday afternoons and evenings.

Beyond Baroque has the largest poetry collection of any bookstore in L.A., and it prides itself on celebrating poetry throughout its life cycle, from a

poem's genesis in a workshop to readings to publication. Free workshops focus on poetry, fiction, or prose; the Mavericks & Masters program gets more in-depth for very modest class fees. The famed Wednesday-night poetry workshop boasts such alums as Wanda Coleman and Tom Waits.

The center also runs poetry contests, art shows, and awards programs, having honored such L.A. lights as Kamau Daáood, Mike Sonksen (aka Mike the Poet), and Eloise Klein Healy. As Venice continues to gentrify to an almost unrecognizable level, it's a comfort to see this graceful, if musty, old Mission-style building remaining a literary beacon...at least for now.

LOS ANGELES
Kamau Daáood

the angels here
have pigeons' wings
blue collars
washed in sweat
the common salt
in tears
tongues swirl
in a stew of cultures
singing asphalt songs
in the midst of seagulls
bebop atop
the San Andreas
a humble plate
of beings

From *The Language of Saxophones* (2015)

THE VENICE CHRONICLES: RAY BRADBURY

IF YOU GIVE ME A DESCRIPTION of a drive, I want to take it. I'm not sure that was true before I moved to Los Angeles, but in this car city, I've often found that the best way to enter the world of a book's protagonist or author is to take the same journey they did. In Ray Bradbury's noir-lite novel *Death Is a Lonely Business*, he provides one such route from downtown L.A. headed west. As a regular downtowner and an eastside dweller, I took that route to get to where the bulk of the action in his novel takes place: Venice Beach.

The novel's nameless narrator is a stand-in for Bradbury, who lived in Venice for several years in the 1940s. Early on in the book, he is driven from the DTLA tenement he used to live in back to Venice by the chauffeur of one of the book's other major characters, Constance Rattigan. Located at the corner of Figueroa and Temple, the tenement is, of course, long gone. Gone, in fact, are all the tenements that filled the neighborhood in the 1930s and '40s, replaced by outcroppings of the large, bland "luxury" apartment buildings with Italianate names that have spread like a fungus. The intersection itself doesn't even exist anymore—Figueroa now goes underneath Temple—but I could take one of the little feeder streets to make the turn westbound onto Temple from Figueroa to begin my journey.

Helpfully, Bradbury describes the route the chauffeur takes: west on Temple to Vermont; south on Vermont to Wilshire; west on Wilshire to Westwood, turning left at a cemetery; south to Venice Boulevard; and Venice to Windward and the home of Constance Rattigan. The route is mostly the same today, other than left turns no longer being allowed from Temple onto Vermont, so off I went.

As I drove down Wilshire, I passed many buildings that would have been showpieces during the novel's era, from the grand white Bryson apartments to the iconic Wiltern theater to the majestic art deco Bullocks Wilshire. The farther west I went, the fewer buildings from that period remained. The speed of the journey is certainly slower now than it was at night in the '40s and '50s, but I obediently followed Bradbury's route, turning south on Sepulveda

Ray Bradbury in 1972; from the L.A. Public Library Archives.

I ran past the little white cottages that came later to nest among the monsters, and the canals that had been dug and filled to mirror the bright skies of 1910 when the white gondolas sailed on clean tides and bridges strung with firefly lightbulbs promised future promenades that arrived like overnight ballet troupes and ran away never to return after the war. And the dark beasts just went on sucking the sand while the gondolas sank, taking the last of some party's laughter with them.

— Ray Bradbury, *Death Is a Lonely Business* (1985)

because it is right by the National Cemetery. Venice and Windward no longer connect, so I parked nearby and set off to explore Venice Beach on foot.

The impetus for the action in *Death Is a Lonely Business* is the closing and demolition of the Venice Pier in 1946. Similar to its neighbor in Santa Monica, the Venice Pier once provided all manner of entertainment, from roller coasters to auditoriums. Santa Monica's pier still thrives, but Venice's is long gone. If you know where to look, however (and you will now know), you can find the most minute traces of it. No signs mention it, but if you go straight out from the foot of Windward onto the sand, you can see where the pier once stood. There was a breakwater at the end to protect it from damage by big surf, and part of that breakwater remains, at the end of a slightly longer spit of beach going into the ocean, just barely marking the footprint of the long-lost pier.

When Bradbury lived here, Venice was derelict. The novel opens with this line: "Venice, California, in the old days had much to recommend it to people who liked to be sad." Now a walk along Abbot Kinney, Pacific, and Windward reveals boutiques selling $200 T-shirts and bistros pouring $20 glasses of wine. Of course, who can see into the hearts of those who stroll the streets of Venice today?

To stay connected with the town of Bradbury's day (and the dead body that instigates the action in *Death Is a Lonely Business*), I made my way to the few canals that are left. Decades ago, many of the canals created by developer Abbot Kinney were filled in and turned into regular streets; the ones that have survived remind us that Venice was given its name for a reason. I walked along the Grand Canal, watching the ducks and looking for the old circus cars abandoned in the water where the dead body is found in the novel. Those are long gone, too, if they weren't just part of the novelist's famously fertile imagination.

The many original houses and small apartment buildings lining Venice's canals and smaller streets make it possible to picture the town as Bradbury and his characters knew it. Sure, they're gussied up and worth a hundred times more than they were in 1946, but it wasn't a stretch for me to recall his vivid descriptions from the novel, like this one: "No one seemed to remember how the canals had gotten there in the middle of an old town somehow fallen to seed, the seeds rustling against the doors every night along with the sand and bits of seaweed and unravelings of tobacco from cigarettes tossing along the strand-shore as far back as 1910."

In the "Brown Room" on the third floor, the Los Angeles Science Fantasy Society met regularly in the 1930s. The group included sci-fi writer/"religion" founder L. Ron Hubbard, famed editor Forrest Ackerman, and a young aspiring writer named Ray Bradbury. Bradbury ate at Clifton's for the rest of his life, and after he passed, his family donated some of his memorabilia, which is displayed on the third floor.

PIERCE BROTHERS WESTWOOD VILLAGE

Next to the Westwood branch of the L.A. Public Library sits a small cemetery isolated from busy Wilshire Boulevard. Pierce Brothers is the final resting place for many a Hollywood celebrity, but members of the city's literary community have been laid to rest there as well. They include Ray Bradbury and his wife, Marguerite; Jackie Collins, who wrote of wealth and celebrity in her popular novels; famed historians Will and Ariel Durant, whose magnum opus is *The Story of Civilization*, and who have an L.A. library branch named for them; Sidney Sheldon, another chronicler of the high-flying life of wealth and stardom; Robert Bloch, Hugo-winning author of the novel (later a movie) *Psycho*; and Danny Sugerman, the former manager of the Doors who wrote several books, including *No One Here Gets Out Alive*.

A couple of unexpected literati buried at Pierce Brothers include Rod McKuen, who moved to Beverly Hills after his poetry career began in the Bay Area, and Truman Capote, whose story is, not surprisingly, complicated. He lived in New York but was very close to Joanna Carson, Johnny Carson's ex-wife, and he died in her Bel-Air home. He left half his ashes to her and half to his partner, Jack Dunphy. Carson's half was stolen during a Halloween party at her house, then mysteriously returned. She was afraid the ashes would be stolen again, so she had them stashed in a crypt at Pierce Brothers. After she died, however (her ashes are in the crypt next to his), her estate removed his ashes and auctioned them off for $43,750. But the empty crypt with his name remains. (To learn more about authors buried here, see page 92.)

The city has grown up immensely around this small cemetery, but its status as a historic site means it will remain a peaceful retreat from the Wilshire Boulevard traffic.

If you need a laugh before you leave, stop by Rodney Dangerfield's grave—the epitaph reads, "There goes the neighborhood."

SAYONARA, LITTLE TOKYO NAOMI HIRAHARA

I MET NAOMI HIRAHARA at Suehiro's, where she sent her characters to eat multiple times in *Sayonara Slam*, one of her seven Mas Arai mysteries. It's a modest, long-running Japanese café in Little Tokyo serving such classics as gyoza, tonkatsu, and udon. We both ordered dishes we love and settled in for a conversation.

Hirahara is easy to talk to, kind and thoughtful and curious. I'd asked her to join me because she's a highly respected member of L.A.'s contemporary mystery-writing community—which is diverse and vibrant, in contrast to that of the hard-boiled era of Raymond Chandler—and I wanted to talk about the often underrepresented communities she writes about, most notably Japanese Americans, and the lesser-known places in greater Los Angeles in which she sets her stories.

Her first mystery series (she's working on a new one now) stars Mas Arai, a Japanese American gardener who lives in Altadena, in the foothills above Pasadena. His work and his nose for unintended sleuthing takes him across the city, but it is in places like Altadena that we discover a world away from the plasticity of Beverly Hills and the garishness of Hollywood. It's a quiet, tree-blanketed community that's ethnically and economically diverse, known for attracting iconoclasts, nature lovers, and people who—like Mas—want to be left alone.

I asked the Altadena native about her history. "I was born Naomi Hirahara," she said. "I have no middle name because I was my mother's firstborn, and Japanese people don't have middle names. She had only been in this country maybe a year and a half. My younger brother has a proper middle name. It kind of shows you the acculturation of my mother."

Mas Arai's origins became clear as we talked about Hirahara's family. "My father's history is very much like Mas's—or, rather, I fashioned Mas's history according to my dad's history," she said. "One reason for that is I really wanted the permission for this to be fiction, but I didn't want people to say, 'Oh, historically that couldn't ever happen.' It did happen to my dad." Her father's journey was unusual. He was born in California to Japanese immigrant parents, who returned to Hiroshima when he was two years old in search of work because the Depression had made jobs in America impossible to find. So he was an American citizen, but he couldn't speak English. Then as a teenager he survived the bomb in Hiroshima, fleeing the ravaged city to return to California in search of work and a new life. Like so many Japanese immigrants of that era, his journey led to farmwork in California's Central Valley, followed by a move to the L.A. area—in her father's case, Altadena—where he found work as a gardener. In Los Angeles from the '20s through the '70s, gardeners were most commonly Japanese American. Many nurseries and florist shops were also run by Japanese Americans.

One of the things I admire about Hirahara's work is her use of Japanese words and culture in a way that is accessible to readers who aren't familiar with them. She explained, "I've been really influenced by people who wrote about the South and used vernacular. And because I was raised in a bilingual household, I think my ear is tuned to figure out what people are trying to say and the rhythms of their dialect."

After discussing the influence of Southern stories and Japanese folktales in her youth, she said, "In my writing, I love history, but I want to document the now. My 'now'—ten, twenty years ago—is already history."

Hirahara is very specific in her writing, giving street names and location descriptions so clearly that I could write a guidebook based solely on her novels. I asked if that comes more from her journalistic background or her desire to make Los Angeles come alive. "I think it's both," she said. "A Japanese scholar once looked at my work and said, 'You write very journalistically,' and at first I wondered if that was an insult. But I've come to understand that it wasn't. It's my journalistic side that makes me really curious about people and places."

Hirahara told me that Suehiro's made it into *Sayonara Slam* because it had been a favorite lunch spot when she worked at *Rafu Shimpo*, L.A.'s Japanese newspaper. "Working there was seminal for me because I'd grown up with a typical suburban, Pasadena-based life, only occasionally going out to other parts of Los Angeles," she said. "At the newspaper, we covered pockets of Japanese Americans all around town. I began to understand community there. One of my goals as a writer is to ground and anchor a place and its relationship to people—so it's

Naomi Hirahara getting her handprints in Vroman's Literary Walk of Fame in 2018.

not just physically describing a place but what it means to the people who live there."

I asked if she writes about place more from memory or from current in-the-field research. "In the Mas books, I thought first in terms of memory," she said, "and then when I'd go visit, I'd find out that it might not fit in with the memory. But that's okay. The way I look at it, it's fiction. Some of my mystery-writing colleagues, if there's no fence in their story and they visit and there's a fence, they'll add a fence. But to me, you never know when that fence is going to come down.

"I don't want to be too specific, and I don't want people to think I'm casting their place in a negative light," she continued. "There are people who have followed my directions and said, 'Naomi, there's nothing like that on Sepulveda.' There comes a point where it becomes imaginary."

Our conversation turned to the neighborhoods in her books. "I like writing about neighborhoods that once had a significant Japanese community but have been changing," Hirahara said. "One is the Crenshaw area—there's still a Japanese American credit union and a senior center there." Other places that are important to her, besides the San Gabriel Valley and Little Tokyo, include Gardena (where Mas's best friend, Haruo, plays poker) and Torrance, but her characters can be found all over L.A. Mas goes to North Hollywood (*Summer of the Big Bachi*) and Montebello (*Blood Hina*) as he investigates murders, his lady friend Genessee lives in Mid-City (*Sayonara Slam* and *Hiroshima Boy*), and Dodger Stadium is pretty much another character in *Sayonara Slam*.

To me, Hirahara's most powerful stories are those involving communities that readers might not have known about before reading her work. To her, that's the fun part: "It's cool to write about places that other people don't."

*It wasn't being refused
employment in the plants so much.
When I got here practically the
only job a Negro could get was
service in the white folks' kitchens.
But it wasn't that so much.
It was the look on
people's faces when
you asked them about
a job. Most of 'em
didn't say right out
they wouldn't hire me.
They just looked so goddamned
startled that I'd even asked.
As if some friendly dog had come
in through the door and said,
"I can talk." It shook me.*

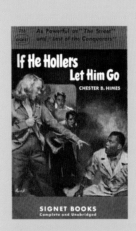

—From *If He Hollers Let Him Go*

CHESTER HIMES

In 2013, the *L.A. Weekly* declared that Chester Himes's debut 1945 novel, *If He Hollers Let Him Go*, was the greatest Los Angeles novel of all time. Notable L.A. poet Mike Sonksen agreed in a piece for KCET. And we're not about to argue. Himes lived and wrote in wartime L.A., and *If He Hollers* follows African American shipyard worker Bob Jones over a few tense days as he copes with various crises around town, from San Pedro to West Adams, Sunset Boulevard to Central Avenue, almost every experience tainted by racism. It was a groundbreaking

work of power and honesty by an African American author. As Sonksen wrote, "Himes set an important precedent with his ability to tell it like it is."

Himes followed up that book in 1947 with another worthy wartime-L.A. novel, *Lonely Crusade*. Several years later, he decamped to live the rest of his life in France and Spain, finding commercial success as an author with his Harlem Detective novels.

NOTES ON A DIRTY OLD MAN CHARLES BUKOWSKI

WHEN APPROACHING THE GEOGRAPHY of legendary bad-boy writer Charles Bukowski, it's hard to resist the pull of Hollywood. His existence there, both lived and fictional, seems vividly real after reading his novels. He even wrote one called *Hollywood*, based on his experiences writing a screenplay. But that seemed too easy; I wanted to explore a part of Los Angeles that he embraced when few other writers did. So I headed to San Pedro.

San Pedro has its roots as a working-class town that supported the Port of Los Angeles, housing longshoremen, fishermen, and cannery workers back when the canneries still operated on Terminal Island, just off San Pedro. It was an immigrant community, attracting Greeks, Croatians, Italians, Portuguese, Mexicans, and Japanese, and to this day you can find Croatian and Italian halls, where people gather with friends from their home countries.

My first stop was the neighborhood in which Bukowski lived. At the time of this writing, his widow, Linda, still resides there, and I didn't want to impinge on her or her ability to live without readers constantly showing up on her doorstep. Instead, using an old *Los Angeles Times* article, I narrowed down his neighborhood to the area around Bandini Street and Bandini Street Elementary School. Near the school is the view of the port that Bukowski loved. It's a solid reminder that this city does not thrive on entertainment and the arts alone—that the largest port in the United States is right here in Los Angeles.

Bukowski wrote about buying his San Pedro house in *Hollywood*: "My tax consultant had suggested I purchase a house, and so for me it wasn't really a matter of 'white flight.'" He also described the house: "It looked like a damned good place to hide. There was even a stairway, an *upstairs* with a bedroom, bathroom, and what was to become my typing room."

The area calls to mind John Fante's character Arturo Bandini in his seminal novel *Ask the Dust*. Fante was a big influence on Bukowski, as he acknowledged in his foreword to *Ask the Dust*. Fante lived in San Pedro when he first came to L.A. and paid homage to it by naming his protagonist Bandini.

> *Hell, L.A. don't go nowhere, and look at this. Shit just comes to us.*
>
> — KAREN TEI YAMASHITA,
> *Tropic of Orange* (1997)

I headed farther into San Pedro toward Green Hills Memorial Park, where Bukowski is buried. A cemetery employee asked for the name of my "loved one," and I felt a little funny replying, "Bukowski." He took it in stride and said he knew exactly where the grave site was. I followed his golf cart to a hillside plot with an orange traffic cone conspicuously sitting on the lawn to mark Bukowski's grave. He gets regular visitors.

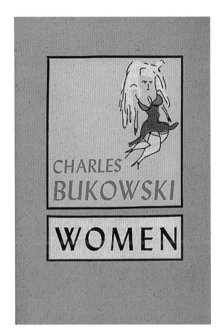

I trudged up the hill and stood at Bukowski's grave, thinking about the hard-drinking man whom *Time* once called the "laureate of American lowlife," whose raw, aggressively masculine poetry, essays, and novels continue to resonate with a global audience decades after his death. It was not long before someone else showed up curbside with a camera, waiting for his turn to pay his literary respects. I left him to it.

The next stop was Hollywood Park. Bukowski played the horses there regularly, and it's impossible to resist the park's importance to him, even though it has changed dramatically since he gambled there. The track closed in 2013, and a new casino opened in 2016. The racetrack has been demolished for the building of a massive football stadium, which was in process as I wrote this, so Bukowski wouldn't recognize any of it. The casino is small compared with the Nevada pleasure palaces, and I quickly found the room with the racetrack betting, remembering when Bukowski's PI protagonist visited Hollywood Park in *Pulp*: "I found myself at the racetrack. Hollywood Park. There were no live horses. They were at Oak Tree. The races were telecast and you bet as usual." I am not a bettor, so I didn't pay admission for the off-track room, but instead ordered a drink and watched the betting action from outside while I drank. Bukowski's habits had to be honored somehow.

Holy the lone juggernaut!
Holy the vast lamb of
the middle class!
Holy the crazy shepherds
of rebellion! Who digs
Los Angeles IS
Los Angeles!

— ALLEN GINSBURG,
Howl and Other Poems (1956)

FROLIC ROOM

Next to the Pantages Theatre, the Frolic Room is Hollywood's oldest bar. It was a speakeasy during Prohibition, starting in 1930, and in 1934 it opened as a proper saloon, then called Bob's Frolic Room. While it has its appeal as a dive bar and a convenient place for a drink before or after a show, its literary connections make it a must-visit for book lovers.

Charles Bukowski parked himself so often on a red-vinyl barstool when he lived in Hollywood in the 1960s and '70s that a picture of him hangs on the wall. He appreciated the joint's convenience and lack of frills, although he didn't write about it the way he did some of his other favorites, leaving it as a more private place to drink. After he died, the bar hosted readings of his work.

The Frolic Room also appeared in the film adaptation of James Ellroy's L.A. noir classic *L.A. Confidential*, and it's notorious for being the last place where Elizabeth Short (aka the Black Dahlia) was seen before she was murdered—a case that inspired another Ellroy novel, *The Black Dahlia*.

And it has one more claim to fame: a mural by the late Al Hirschfeld, whose caricatures of famous figures appeared regularly in the drama section of *The New York Times*. He became internationally known, publishing such books as *Hirschfeld's Hollywood*, which captures work he did for the film studios.

It is hard to describe, now, the heady atmosphere of those first few years of Hollywood. The modest film operations of New York City had moved to the wider, warmer region of Los Angeles, where, like seedlings suddenly exposed to water and light, they shot up and flourished unchecked.

— NINA REVOYR,
The Age of Dreaming (2008)

The circa-1926 Hollywood Roosevelt was as glamorous as Hollywood itself in its 1930s and '40s heyday, but like so many young stars, it didn't age well. Fortunately, thanks to a couple of restorations and protective status as a Los Angeles Historical-Cultural Monument, it's now as ageless as Paul Rudd. Take your book to the wood-paneled, leather-sofaed Library Bar, order a Negroni, and channel such former guests as Ernest Hemingway, F. Scott Fitzgerald, and William Faulkner, who was known for occasionally reciting drunken Shakespeare in the bar. Fun fact: Bestselling author/astrologer Linda Goodman wrote several books while living in a suite here.

DREAMING OF BUNKER HILL
JOHN FANTE

ARTURO BANDINI FIRST APPEARS in John Fante's *Wait Until Spring, Bandini*, but it is in *Ask the Dust*, Fante's best-known novel, that most readers meet him. In the 1939 classic, young Bandini moves from Colorado to downtown L.A. to become a writer. Bandini's L.A.—whose residents are just barely getting by during the tail end of the Depression—is a little seedier and a lot less privileged than what we mostly see in DTLA now (not counting the significant homeless population).

Fante himself lived downtown in his early days in L.A., and his realistic details pepper the novel, making it easy to picture Bandini's haunts. The changing nature of the city means that many of the locations from the 1930s are gone or transformed, of course, but I set out to find as much as I could.

I began my Fante exploration at the covered Grand Central Market, where Bandini goes to look at "the Mexican girls," who intimidated him. ("They were Aztec princesses and Mayan princesses, the peon girls in the Grand Central Market, in the Church of Our Lady, and I even went to Mass to look at them.") The food hall has changed immensely from Bandini and Fante's day. At first it was as stylish and upscale as it is now, but by the late Depression and postwar period, it had become more of a place for bargain produce, which is what it still was when I started working downtown in 2009. Now the gentrified century-old market is again packed with foodie destinations, though a few holdouts (like Chiles Secos) remain, helping make it possible to picture Bandini and his Aztec princesses meandering through the tightly packed passages.

Across Hill Street from the market is Angels Flight, the shortest railway in the world. The funicular was built to ferry Bunker Hill residents up the hill with their shopping, but now it's just a fun way to experience old downtown. When Fante lived there, Angels Flight ran up the hillside where the Third Street tunnel now goes under the hill.

Today's Grand Central Market, glossed up for the Instagram era.

Los Angeles, give me some of you! Los Angeles come to me the way I came to you, my feet over your streets, you pretty town I loved you so much, you sad flower in the sand, you pretty town!

— JOHN FANTE, *Ask the Dust* (1939)

The funicular was removed in 1969 to allow for the tunnel's construction and rebuilt in its current location in 1996, making it that most L.A. of landmarks: one that has been changed and replaced to serve a fast-growing metropolis.

I took Angels Flight to the top and wandered around the developments that completely replaced the old Bunker Hill. The ride is so short, it feels unnecessary, but I enjoyed imagining it full of well-heeled residents from the era before Fante's, when the hill's Victorian houses were elegant and had not yet become the tenements of Bandini's story. Bandini lived in a residential hotel, the Alta Loma, built into the side of Bunker Hill, an area now flanked along Olive Street by giant retirement complexes with great views of the city.

I followed Bandini's route from the opening of *Ask the Dust*: "I walked down Olive Street past a dirty yellow apartment house that was still wet like a blotter from last night's fog." Those old apartment houses are long gone, replaced by 1980s skyscraper progress. "And so I was down on 5th and Olive, where the big street cars chewed your ears with their noise and the smell of gasoline made the sight of the palm trees seem sad." There are neither streetcars nor palms left at this intersection. "So now I was in front of the Biltmore Hotel, walking along the line of yellow cabs…. I was passing the doorman of the Biltmore and I hated him at once." I, too, walked past the Biltmore, a gem of old downtown that still gleams today. I watched for fancy people to arrive, like the ones Bandini saw, but was faced with normal, upscale twenty-first-century hotel guests, no one stepping out of the past in furs and jewels.

Up 5th Street from the Biltmore is the Central Library (see page 82). The magnificent building was restored after a massive fire in 1986, so while it retains the essence of its 1930s design, it has been greatly modernized. (Susan Orlean's *The Library Book* is an excellent document of the fire and its legacy.) Bandini visits its stacks to find where his books would be shelved when he gets published. I followed his lead and walked through the fiction section, stopping in the *Bs* to locate where his fictional books would have lived, then progressed to the *F*s to find Fante's actual books. Most of them were checked out—he remains popular among Angelenos.

My last stop at the library was the historical archives, to learn more about Bandini's L.A.; I discovered that the Columbia Buffet, where love/hate interest Camilla Lopez works, didn't exist. Walking down to Spring Street, I looked for remnants of the secondhand booksellers that Bandini explores en route to the Columbia Buffet, but today, the only used bookstore on Spring is the Last Bookstore, which didn't open until 2011 in its current location—a grand, circa-1914 former bank building that Bandini (and Fante) would have passed by regularly.

One block over is Main Street, which I took to follow Bandini's progress to Olvera Street. Imagining Bandini striding through downtown, driven by his hubris and longing for something to change his young life, lent a feeling of importance and encouragement to my sweat-inducing walk up Main Street under a hot summer sun. Olvera Street has been revitalized and preserved, almost as a Disneyland of L.A.'s Mexican history. No prostitutes hang around the plaza, as they did in Fante's time; now vendors sell embroidered dresses and taquitos and leather bags. Being there, among the historic buildings of El Pueblo de Los Angeles, I was struck with the eternal promise of this far-west American outpost, a promise that so profoundly motivated both Fante and his alter ego, Arturo Bandini.

King Eddy, at 5th and Los Angeles, remains pleasantly ungentrified to this day. Bukowski was a regular, and if you're seeking the feel of Fante's downtown, you can't do better.

ONCE UPON AN L.A. WRITER

Most of these authors are no longer among the living. At this writing, Joan Didion, David Ebershoff, Thomas Pynchon, and Joseph Wambaugh are still very much alive, but they no longer live in the Los Angeles area.

AUTHOR ➤ WHERE? ➤ KNOWN FOR

L. FRANK BAUM ➤ Hollywood ➤ The Wizard of Oz

RAY BRADBURY ➤ Cheviot Hills / Venice ➤ The Martian Chronicles

CARLOS BULOSAN ➤ Bunker Hill ➤ America Is in the Heart

EDGAR RICE BURROUGHS ➤ Malibu / Hollywood / Beverly Hills ➤ The Tarzan books

OCTAVIA E. BUTLER ➤ Pasadena ➤ Kindred

JAMES M. CAIN ➤ Hollywood ➤ Double Indemnity

BEBE MOORE CAMPBELL ➤ Unknown ➤ Your Blues Ain't Like Mine

CARLOS CASTANEDA ➤ Westwood ➤ Journey to Ixtlan

RAYMOND CHANDLER ➤ Hollywood / Los Angeles / Reseda / Santa Monica / Pacific Palisades ➤ The Big Sleep

EILEEN CHANG ➤ Westwood ➤ Lust, Caution

JULIA CHILD ➤ Pasadena ➤ My Life in France

ELDRIDGE CLEAVER ➤ East L.A. ➤ Soul on Ice

WANDA COLEMAN ➤ Watts / various parts of L.A. ➤ Heavy Daughter Blues

JOAN DIDION ➤ Brentwood Park ➤ Play It as It Lays / The White Album

HARRIET DOERR ➤ Pasadena ➤ Stones for Ibarra

WILL & ARIEL DURANT ➤ Westwood / West L.A. / Los Feliz ➤ The Story of Civilization

DAVID EBERSHOFF ➤ Pasadena ➤ The 19th Wife

L. Frank Baum

Julia Child

Charlotte Perkins Gilman

Lillian Hellman & Dashiell Hammett

Langston Hughes

Aldous Huxley

Carolyn See

Tennessee Williams

JOHN FANTE ➤ Bunker Hill ➤ Ask the Dust

WILLIAM FAULKNER ➤ Santa Monica / Culver City / Hollywood / Beverly Hills ➤ The Sound and the Fury

RICHARD FEYNMAN ➤ Pasadena ➤ Surely You're Joking, Mr. Feynman!

M.F.K. FISHER ➤ Whittier / Eagle Rock / Highland Park / Laguna ➤ Serve It Forth

F. SCOTT FITZGERALD ➤ Garden of Allah / Encino / Hollywood ➤ The Great Gatsby

ERLE STANLEY GARDNER ➤ Ventura / Temecula / Hollywood / Idyllwild ➤ Perry Mason books

CHARLOTTE PERKINS GILMAN ➤ Pasadena ➤ The Yellow Wallpaper

JONATHAN GOLD ➤ Pasadena / various parts of L.A. ➤ Counter Intelligence

ZANE GREY ➤ Altadena ➤ Riders of the Purple Sage

DASHIELL HAMMETT ➤ Garden of Allah / Beverly Hills / Bel-Air ➤ The Maltese Falcon

LILLIAN HELLMAN ➤ Garden of Allah ➤ The Little Foxes

CHESTER HIMES ➤ Unknown ➤ If He Hollers Let Him Go

LANGSTON HUGHES ➤ South L.A. ➤ Montage of a Dream Deferred

ALDOUS HUXLEY ➤ Hollywood / Pacific Palisades ➤ Brave New World

CHRISTOPHER ISHERWOOD ➤ Hollywood / Santa Monica ➤ A Single Man

ROBINSON JEFFERS ➤ Eagle Rock / Manhattan Beach / Highland Park ➤ Robinson Jeffers: Selected Poems

SINCLAIR LEWIS ➤ Chateau Marmont / Beverly Hills Hotel / Beverly Hills ➤ Elmer Gantry

MALCOLM LOWRY ➤ Virgil Village ➤ Under the Volcano

NORMAN MAILER ➤ Laurel Canyon ➤ The Naked and the Dead

THOMAS MANN ➤ Pacific Palisades ➤ The Magic Mountain

W. SOMERSET MAUGHAM ➤ Garden of Allah ➤ Of Human Bondage

ARTHUR MILLER ➤ Beverly Hills Hotel ➤ Death of a Salesman

HENRY MILLER ➤ Beverly Glen / Santa Monica / Pacific Palisades ➤ Tropic of Cancer

ANAÏS NIN ➤ Silver Lake ➤ A Spy in the House of Love

DOROTHY PARKER ➤ Garden of Allah / Hollywood ➤ The Portable Dorothy Parker

S.J. PERELMAN ➤ Beverly Hills / Garden of Allah ➤ Westward Ha!

KATHERINE ANNE PORTER ➤ Beverly Hills Hotel ➤ Ship of Fools

THOMAS PYNCHON ➤ The South Bay ➤ The Crying of Lot 49

AYN RAND ➤ Hollywood / San Fernando Valley ➤ The Fountainhead

WILL ROGERS ➤ Pacific Palisades / Beverly Hills ➤ The Cowboy Philosopher

CAROLYN SEE ➤ Eagle Rock / Topanga Canyon / Santa Monica ➤ Golden Days

UPTON SINCLAIR ➤ Pasadena ➤ The Jungle

JOHN STEINBECK ➤ Eagle Rock / Hermosa Beach ➤ The Grapes of Wrath

IRVING STONE ➤ Beverly Hills ➤ Lust for Life

GORE VIDAL ➤ Hollywood Hills ➤ Myra Breckenridge / United States: Essays 1952–1992

JOSEPH WAMBAUGH ➤ L.A. area ➤ The Onion Field / The Choirboys

NATHANAEL WEST ➤ Hollywood ➤ The Day of the Locust

TENNESSEE WILLIAMS ➤ Santa Monica ➤ Sweet Bird of Youth

HERMAN WOUK ➤ Garden of Allah ➤ The Caine Mutiny

Such sacred ordinariness implies a sense of what has come before, which is one of the stories downtown tells me. It is readable in the lines of the streets, the quick passage from Bunker Hill through Grand Central Market and out to Broadway, where the Bradbury building is both landmark and commercial space. This is it, the double vision, the layering that, increasingly, I see everywhere.

— David L. Ulin, *Sidewalking* (2015)

IN THE NOT QUITE NEW DOWNTOWN

DANA JOHNSON

SEVERAL OF DANA JOHNSON'S short stories from her 2016 collection, *In the Not Quite Dark*, revolve around the Pacific Electric Building, which was once a terminus for streetcars in downtown Los Angeles. Cole's, which claims (along with Philippe's) to have invented the French dip, has occupied the ground floor of that building since 1908, and inside it glows with the atmosphere of the early twentieth century. Dimly lit, with dark wood and etched glass, it serves lunchtime French dips and after-work cocktails to downtown folks, and it's where Johnson and I met for a happy-hour talk about her writing and her city.

A professor in USC's PhD creative writing program, she writes about African American narratives in L.A. in a way that is distinctly her own. Her 2012 debut novel, *Elsewhere, California* shows in brilliant detail how moving from Watts to West Covina shapes Avery, the story's protagonist. It is a journey based on Johnson's own childhood experience of moving out to the suburbs after violence hit too close to home. Though, as Johnson was quick to point out, Avery's story is fiction, not a memoir.

"When I started writing seriously," she said, "I thought about how, in all the books I'd read about L.A., I never saw myself as a black, middle-class, suburban person. I thought those experiences weren't important. It wasn't about Hollywood or something sexy—but then I realized that West Covina *is* suitable material, especially the story of moving from an all-black neighborhood to somewhere predominantly white." Her ability to push past the typical Hollywood-centered images of L.A. to explore the everyday experience of unrecognized neighborhoods is part of what makes Johnson's work so powerful.

"We already know about Hollywood," she explained. So her stories hew more closely to her own personal geography, whether it's the eastern suburbs of *Elsewhere, California* or the downtown of *In the Not Quite Dark*. "I'm interested in a bigger view of Los Angeles and its suburbs," she

Photo by Ellie Partovi

said. "I want to read those stories too. I don't want to just write them."

Johnson went to grad school in Bloomington, Indiana, an experience that made her realize how much she connected with her city. "I love L.A. so much, and I've never felt as comfortable anywhere else," she said. "I'd come home and feel like a tourist: 'Look at the mountains, they're beautiful! Let's go to the beach!' It felt so novel because I was no longer living here. When you live somewhere else, like the Midwest—and there are aspects of it I loved—I really understood what I missed about Los Angeles and what I loved about it. I felt it bodily." Moving back to L.A. affected her writing as well as her appreciation for the city. "Doing my MFA in Bloomington was amazing, and it saved my life, but being in L.A. has been great for my writing."

L.A.'s literary community plays into Johnson's love for her city, and it's an important aspect of her writing process. She tries to attend readings as often as possible, but admitted, "I feel like a bad literary citizen sometimes because I cannot go to all of the readings. There are so many, and I just can't do it all. It's an embarrassment of riches, and it negates the image of Los Angeles where nothing is happening on the literary scene. A *lot* is happening, all the time." She's also involved in a writing group. "It's helpful to have people who will read my work. Writing is such a weird thing—increasingly, nobody cares that you write. You're doing it because you're doing it. Whenever you can find support, which is easy to do in this city, it's very doable." Being able to give and receive that support is an essential part of her writing life

Of the geography she describes, Johnson said, "Whenever I've written about home, I feel it's really important to be specific and accurate about the details of the people and the spaces. However, since *In the Not Quite Dark* came out, so much of the city is so different from what I wrote. I was very careful to get the details right then, but it's not the same downtown now." One example, she said, is Grand Central Market, which was renovated and repopulated after she wrote the book. "To me, it reflected the diversity of downtown. But now it's sort of generic. You used to walk into an amazing experience of culture and food. My dad is eighty-

> *But before Main Street had changed on Dean, it had changed on so many others before him, people who had lived there for years before he'd even heard of downtown.*
>
> — DANA JOHNSON,
> *In the Not Quite Dark* (2016)

three. He's from Tennessee and migrated to California. He came to visit me downtown and wanted to go to Grand Central Market. There was a fish market he loved downstairs, so we went and it was gone."

Downtown also indirectly provided inspiration for Johnson's story about Biddy Mason in *In the Not Quite Dark*. "I came across her through the artwork that's behind Maccheroni Republic and Wells Fargo and a dry cleaner," she recalled. "I walk all the time, and I was just walking down Broadway and came across it. I didn't know anything about this woman. I'd already started writing about Henry Huntington. But once I started learning about Biddy Mason, I became really interested in talking about a well-known white Los Angeles figure versus an African American woman who was not as well-known but made major contributions to this city. It was all accidental."

Giving voice to lesser-known historical figures, as well as to communities that rarely see themselves on the page, are among the most beautiful elements of Johnson's work. She added, "I think it's important to get things right for what they were, even if they inevitably change." She might have been referring just to geography, but it's also an ethos for how she captures the spirit of the people and places she writes about.

Los Angeles: nineteen suburbs in search of a metropolis.

— H.L. MENCKEN, in *Photoplay*

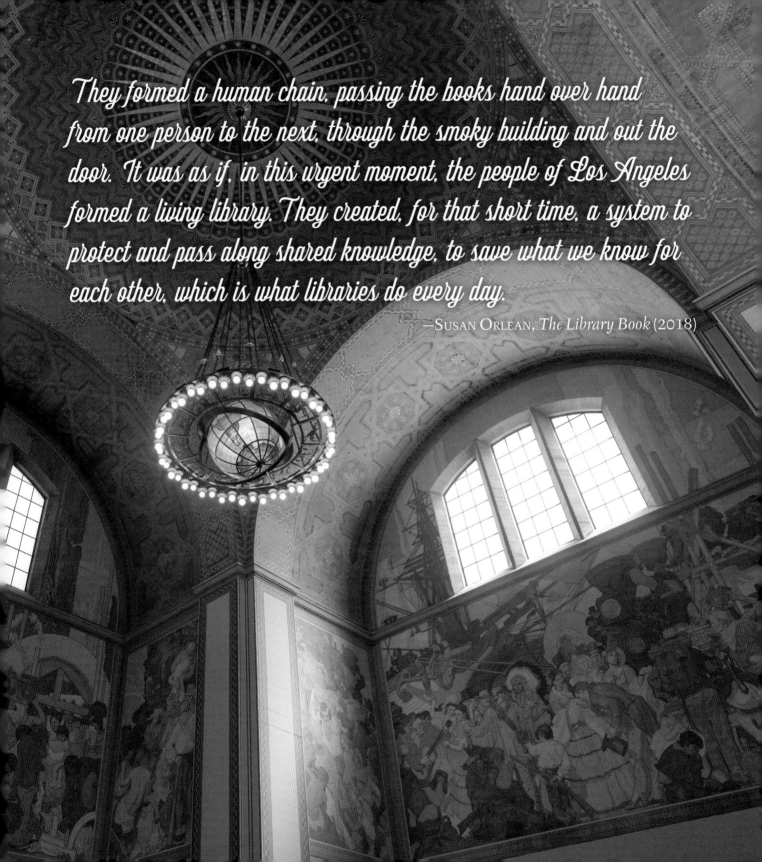

They formed a human chain, passing the books hand over hand from one person to the next, through the smoky building and out the door. It was as if, in this urgent moment, the people of Los Angeles formed a living library. They created, for that short time, a system to protect and pass along shared knowledge, to save what we know for each other, which is what libraries do every day.

—SUSAN ORLEAN, *The Library Book* (2018)

LOS ANGELES CENTRAL LIBRARY

Susan Orlean's bestseller *The Library Book* has made a national star out of the Los Angeles Central Library, but to locals, it's long been the heart of the city's book-loving community. It's where Ray Bradbury borrowed typewriters to write his early works, where Octavia E. Butler conducted research and read for pleasure, and where John Fante's fictional Arturo Bandini stalked its stacks, looking for where works by the great Bandini would be shelved one day.

The downtown HQ for a sprawling system of seventy-three branches, the Bertram Goodhue–designed building dates to 1926, with a mosaic pyramid tower that echoes City Hall. After the devastating 1986 fire that Orlean details in her book, it was restored and enlarged to a dazzling degree—from the grand California-history murals, to the exterior art deco sculptures, to the Mark Taper Auditorium, to the terraced, cypress-lined gardens, it's an even more cherished landmark today than it was decades ago.

The fire destroyed hundreds of thousands of books (including a vast treasure trove of cookbooks), but some collections have been rebuilt, and today the library is home to, among many other riches, a photo collection that numbers in the millions, as well as deep collections of maps, sheet music, monographs, Californiana, fruit-crate labels, menus, movie posters, children's books, and literature.

Of course, community events are plentiful, both at the Central Library and at the branches: storytimes, art exhibits, literacy classes, teen book clubs, financial-literacy programs, and much, much more.

JOSH KUN is one of L.A.'s most valuable archivists, and he's produced a number of books on music, history, and culture. Two of his most beautiful titles celebrate two particularly rich collections of the L.A. Central Library: *To Live and Dine in L.A.: Menus and the Making of the Modern City*, and *Songs in the Key of Los Angeles*, written with Van Dyke Parks. Both are from hometown publisher Angel City Press, and both are well worth deep dives into the collections.

A FEW ESSENTIAL LIBRARIES

HUNTINGTON LIBRARY

One of the nation's literary treasures, this grand collection is part of the Huntington Library, Art Collections, and Botanical Gardens in San Marino. The museum area of the library features such rarities as Audubon's *Birds of America*, the Ellesmere manuscript of Chaucer's *Canterbury Tales*, the Gutenberg Bible, and some of the first versions of Shakespeare's plays ever printed. Those stars are usually on view, and other items from the collection of more than nine million pieces rotate in and out of the display cases.

Huntington Library's main exhibition hall; photo courtesy Huntington Library.

Alas, if you want to do a deep dive into the papers of Evelyn Waugh, Paul Theroux, Charles Bukowski, Octavia E. Butler, or Hilary Mantel—not to mention the astonishing collections of history (American, Hispanic, Californian, Pacific Rim, and British), literature, maps, medieval manuscripts, photography, ephemera, and more—you'll have to get qualified as a scholar/researcher, known here as a "reader." Life goal.

PASADENA CENTRAL LIBRARY

Built as part of Pasadena's Civic Center development in the 1920s, this Spanish Renaissance structure is on the National Register of Historic Places. The inside reflects elegance and quiet inquiry, with high ceilings and long wooden tables in the central hub; a wonderful children's room containing upward of 60,000 books, videos, and magazines; a handsome auditorium that hosts author events and screenings; a coffee bar; and strong collections of business, general reference, periodicals, and Pasadena history.

Studiousness in the Pasadena Central Library; photo by Keegan Dunn.

Frank Gehry fancifulness at the Hollywood Library.

In the infinite city, a legion of men and women stock, service, and warm up thousands of taco trucks in the truck yards, in the steam, in the fluorescent lights cutting the dark in the other side of chainlink fence.

— SESSHU FOSTER,
City of the Future (2018)

SANTA MONICA MAIN LIBRARY

Unlike the classics found in Pasadena and at UCLA, this 2006 building is modern, airy, and bright, with a cheerful café and lots of computer services. It's a destination thanks to its outstanding auditorium, which hosts author events, movie screenings, and lectures. The library also organizes a series of book clubs and kids' programs, and the collections are strong in languages and Santa Monica history and literature.

FRANCES HOWARD GOLDWYN HOLLYWOOD REGIONAL LIBRARY

Back in 1985, when Frank Gehry was just becoming a big deal, he designed this building to replace the beloved old one that had burned down a few years earlier. It was financed by the Samuel Goldwyn Foundation and named for Goldwyn Sr.'s wife, whose formal education ended at age fourteen but who became a scholar of English and French history by reading in libraries. The entertainment community chipped in to help rebuild the collections lost in the fire, and now it has fabulous archives of rare books with Hollywood themes (many from the libraries of Hollywood icons; yes, they read books), along with historic screenplays and teleplays, Hollywood history, silent-film memorabilia, and movie posters.

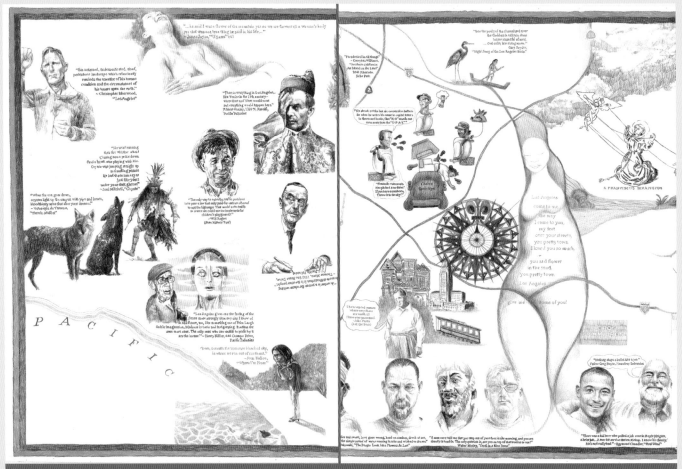

Details from J. Michael Walker's *City in Mind* mural at Powell Library.

POWELL LIBRARY, UCLA

Modeled on Milan's Basilica of Sant'Ambrogio, this gorgeous late-1920s library is one of the showpieces of the UCLA campus. Its literary history is rich: It was named for famed author and UCLA librarian Lawrence Clark Powell, and Ray Bradbury wrote *Fahrenheit 451* in its basement. The library not only holds Bradbury's papers, but also those of such writers as Raymond Chandler, Wanda Coleman, and Anaïs Nin.

But the hands-down reason you must visit is to see artist J. Michael Walker's fantastic twenty-three-foot-long literary map of Los Angeles, which the Special Collections department acquired from Libros Schmibros in 2013. Called *City in Mind: A Lyrical Map of the City of Los Angeles*, it's a wonder for readers and history buffs alike. You'll find it in the library's stacks.

KINDRED SPIRITS
OCTAVIA E. BUTLER

SOME OF OCTAVIA E. BUTLER'S Los Angeles can be found in her fiction: *Kindred* has characters who live in Altadena, *Parable of the Sower* begins in a post-apocalyptic wasteland version of L.A., and *Mind of My Mind* is set in a fictional L.A. suburb. Despite her large body of work, however, it's difficult to trace much of the Pasadena native's experience in her writing because most of the stories take place elsewhere, including outer space—she did, after all, write science fiction. With this limitation in mind, I decided to focus on her personal geography.

The Huntington Library in San Marino was the logical starting place. It acquired Butler's extensive papers and key belongings after she died in 2006, and it's a rich collection that attracts scholars every year. Although there are no permanent displays of her work alongside the Gutenberg Bible or the manuscript of Jack London's *The Sea-Wolf*, the library put on an exhibition of her work in 2017, and I made sure to visit. Seeing her notebooks and pictures of Butler in her youth gave me background and understanding that added depth to my reading of her fiction, not to mention clues identifying locations from her life in Pasadena and Altadena to explore.

Butler grew up in sharp contrast to the wealth on display at the opulent library and vast gardens of Henry Huntington's San Marino estate. The daughter of a maid (her father died when she was a baby), she was a shy, tall, awkward African American girl in a racially mixed, north Pasadena neighborhood. She attended Pasadena public schools, graduating from John Muir High and Pasadena City College. The disparity between her works' current home at the luxe Huntington and her working-class roots a few miles away calls to mind her descriptions of the fictional suburb of Robledo in *Parable of the Sower*. "Robledo—twenty miles from Los Angeles, and, according to Dad, once a rich, green, unwalled little city" stands apart from her depiction of the fictional 2024 wreckage of Los Angeles, functioning as a metaphor for the socioeconomic gulf between San Marino and the poorer parts of L.A.

A few blocks north of the Huntington is PCC, Butler's alma mater. I walked the lovely small

> *Los Angeles forms and shatters, forms and shatters.*
>
> — OCTAVIA E. BUTLER, from a notebook in the Huntington collection

Octavia Butler's yearbook photo from Muir High in Pasadena.

campus like she once did, noting how much the voracious reader would have appreciated the gorgeous, relatively new library that is now the centerpiece of the college and wondering how her classes there influenced her as a writer. (She continued to study writing after her time at PCC, attending writers' and screenwriters' workshops in Los Angeles and elsewhere.)

Northwest of PCC is the Pasadena Central Library, where Butler spent much of her childhood reading. Solitary by nature, she found her home in books, and because her mother couldn't afford to buy them, she'd drop her very young daughter off at the Italianate, Myron Hunt–designed 1924 landmark library on her way to work. Butler would sit for hours in the children's room, reading book after book. As she got older, she'd take the bus or walk to the library. As I wandered through the stacks, it was easy to picture her doing the same—little has changed at this historic library. In the stately Centennial Room, I searched the shelves of Pasadena authors and found only a copy of her book *Imago*. I did a quick search of the catalog and discovered that most of Butler's work is shelved elsewhere in the building—and that day, most of the copies were checked out, a reflection of the continuing devotion the local community has for her. I found myself wishing the library would create some sort of tribute; in 2017, it staged a celebration in honor of her 70th birthday, but something more permanent seems more than appropriate.

Butler's life directed me next a couple of miles north to Altadena, the hometown of Dana and Kevin from *Kindred*. I drove past Victorian homes and snug bungalows like the one I imagined them living in on my way to Mountain View Cemetery, where Butler's grave sits in a peaceful island of grass and gravestones. Her simple headstone is adorned with the central verse from *Parable of the Sower*:

All that you touch
You Change.

All that you Change
Changes you.

The only lasting truth
Is Change.

God
Is Change.

On a late Sunday afternoon, there weren't many people visiting the cemetery, and I was able to have a quiet moment at her grave, reflecting on her work and legacy.

In one day, I stopped at both resting places of Octavia E. Butler: her body resides at Mountain View Cemetery; her spirit and work live on at the Huntington Library. How fortunate we are that she bequeathed her archives to the world-class institution next door to her hometown.

Octavia Butler's resting place: Mountain View Cemetery in Altadena.

RIP: AUTHOR BURIAL SITES

If you'd like to pay your respects to a literary hero who's moved on to the Great Beyond, here are some cemeteries to visit. Most are also quiet, green retreats peacefully removed from L.A.'s traffic and concrete. (See also the sidebar on Pierce Brothers on page 64.)

EVERGREEN CEMETERY

➤ H.T. Tsiang ➤ The Hanging on Union Square

FOREST LAWN GLENDALE

➤ Forrest Ackerman ➤ A Reference Guide to American Science Fiction Films
➤ L. Frank Baum ➤ The Wonderful Wizard of Oz
➤ Vincent Bugliosi ➤ Helter Skelter
➤ W.R. Burnett ➤ Little Caesar
➤ Lloyd C. Douglas ➤ Magnificent Obsession

L. Frank Baum is only one of many notable writers buried at Forest Lawn Glendale.

- Theodore Dreiser ➤ An American Tragedy
- Louis L'Amour ➤ more than 100 books, including Hopalong Cassidy
- Johnston McCulley ➤ creator of Zorro
- Adela Rogers St. Johns ➤ Final Verdict
- Jim Tully ➤ Shanty Irish

Charles Bukowski's resting place in San Pedro.

FOREST LAWN HOLLYWOOD HILLS
- John Dudley Ball ➤ In the Heat of the Night
- Carrie Fisher ➤ Postcards from the Edge
- Michelle McNamara ➤ I'll Be Gone in the Dark
- Paul Monette ➤ Borrowed Time

GREEN HILLS MEMORIAL PARK
- Charles Bukowski ➤ Women

HILLSIDE MEMORIAL PARK
- Julia Phillips ➤ You'll Never Eat Lunch in This Town Again
- Irving Wallace ➤ The Prize

HOLLYWOOD FOREVER
- Norman Cousins ➤ The Human Adventure
- Jonathan Gold ➤ Counter Intelligence

HOLY CROSS CEMETERY
- John Fante ➤ Ask the Dust
- Gene Fowler ➤ Skyline
- Jim Murray ➤ The Jim Murray Reader

INGLEWOOD PARK CEMETERY
- Bebe Moore Campbell ➤ Brothers and Sisters

MOUNTAIN VIEW CEMETERY

➤ Octavia E. Butler ➤ Kindred

➤ Richard Feynman ➤ Surely You're Joking, Mr. Feynman

PIERCE BROTHERS WESTWOOD VILLAGE

➤ Robert Bloch ➤ Psycho

➤ Ray Bradbury ➤ Fahrenheit 451

➤ Truman Capote ➤ In Cold Blood

➤ Jackie Collins ➤ Hollywood Wives

➤ Kate Coscarelli ➤ Fame and Fortune

➤ Sidney Sheldon ➤ The Other Side of Midnight

➤ Alvin Toffler ➤ Future Shock

TARZAN IN TARZANA

Yes, the Valley suburb of Tarzana really was named for Tarzan the Ape Man. In 1919, Edgar Rice Burroughs, the fabulously successful author of the Tarzan novels, bought a 550-acre ranch from *L.A. Times* publisher Harrison Gray Otis for $120,000 and named it Tarzana Ranch. Burroughs was as savvy a real estate investor as he was a writer—he made another pile in the 1920s by subdividing his ranch and selling off lots for the new community.

After he died in 1950, his ashes were buried under the walnut tree in the front yard of his Tarzana office, at 18354 Ventura Boulevard—where Edgar Rice Burroughs Inc. is based to this day.

SLEEPY LAGOON POR VIDA LUIS VALDEZ

SLEEPY LAGOON NO LONGER EXISTS. Where it once stood on the Williams Ranch in Commerce there are now warehouses, train tracks, and a power station. Nothing marks the small reservoir where people came to swim and party. Nothing commemorates that a murder at Sleepy Lagoon in 1942 led to one of the biggest racial injustices in L.A. history. Perhaps the city prefers it that way.

It is remembered, however, because Luis Valdez wrote *Zoot Suit*. His play about the murder and the subsequent trial, which unfairly targeted large numbers of Chicano youths, many of whom were associated with the 38th Street Gang, tells the story of these pachucos and the Zoot Suit riots in a dynamic, powerful way. It was an immediate sensation when it premiered at L.A.'s Mark Taper Forum in 1978, and in 1979 it became the first Chicano-written and Chicano-focused play on Broadway, making a star of Edward James Olmos. Its success on Broadway led to the 1981 feature film, which Valdez himself directed.

After reading several of Valdez's plays, I set out to visit key locations in Mexican American Los Angeles that he has featured, as well as theaters in which his work has been performed.

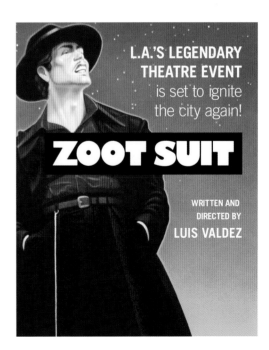

L.A.'S LEGENDARY THEATRE EVENT is set to ignite the city again!

ZOOT SUIT

WRITTEN AND DIRECTED BY **LUIS VALDEZ**

He began as a playwright with El Teatro Campesino in Northern California, but many of his works—*Zoot Suit*, *Bandido!*, *I Don't Have to Show You No Stinking Badges!*— take place in Mexican American communities in the greater L.A. area.

My first stop was Sleepy Lagoon, only to find there weren't any traces of it left. Like most of Southern California's former ranchland, it's paved over and developed. This particular spot, in Commerce just south of East Los Angeles, has long been bordered by communities with large Latinx populations.

I drove north from Commerce into East L.A. and then headed west along Cesar E. Chavez Avenue. El Teatro Campesino was founded to produce plays for and about the farmworkers whom Chavez organized and fought for. Sometimes performances were staged on the backs of trucks in the fields. The street named for him goes through Boyle Heights, a diverse and rapidly (and controversially) gentrifying neighborhood, and into the northern part of downtown.

I passed Olvera Street and its re-created Mexican history and turned south toward the Los Angeles Theatre Center, which has produced many of Valdez's plays, including *I Don't Have to Show You No Stinking Badges!* It's one of downtown's many repurposed buildings, with a beautiful lobby and three theaters of various sizes, which allow for productions of different scales to find a home in the heart of the Historic Core.

Walking north from the LATC to the Music Center, I passed by the former *Los Angeles Times* building. The city's journalism hub for more than eighty years, it stands empty since the staff relocated to El Segundo in 2018. I thought of the recurring newspaper motif in *Zoot Suit* and the way in which coverage of the trial of Henry Leyvas and his compatriots for the murder of José Gallardo Díaz fueled discontent both in the play and in real life.

No second chances in the land of a thousand dances, the valley of ten million insanities.

— RY COODER,
Los Angeles Stories (2011)

Up Bunker Hill from the old *Times* building is the complex of theaters that make up the Music Center. Inside the Ahmanson Theatre lobby, a banner snakes around the walls, telling visitors about historic performances. Among them are pictures of *Zoot Suit*'s premiere, and happily for my particular exploration that day, there happened to be a display of costumes from the original production, as well as information about the revival the theater hosted in 2017.

In 2018, Valdez's *Valley of the Heart* was staged at the Mark Taper Forum (another Music Center venue), and while it is not set in L.A., it gave me a chance to see Valdez's work the way it is meant to be enjoyed: as a live performance. The Center Theatre Group's continued commitment to Valdez will hopefully make that possible for many more years to come.

An easy ride on the Metro Red Line from downtown to Universal City took me from the venues where Valdez's work is performed to a place in which he set one of his plays. *Bandido!* portrays the life of a Californio rebel, Tiburcio Vásquez, and is set a few decades after Mexico surrendered California to the United States with the treaty of Guadalupe Hidalgo.

Bandido! stands as a counterpoint to the earliest Los Angeles novel, *Ramona*, and its romanticism of Mexican and Native American life in Southern California. Helen Hunt Jackson had good intentions in writing about the difficulty of the European-American annexation of California and the loss of land and culture for those who had lived there for generations (in the case of the Mexican Californios) or millennia (in the case of the San Ysidros and Gabrielinos), but Valdez provides a more realized, "own voices" story of the era.

At the Universal City Metro stop, the art adorning the platform's columns tells the story of the Campo de Cahuenga and the treaty that was struck there by American and Mexican forces to end the war over California. It might seem strange to suggest visiting a subway platform to connect with history, but I was grateful that Metro chose to showcase this story in the very place it had happened.

An escalator ride to street level put me just outside the actual Campo de Cahuenga, where the treaty that preceded the Treaty of Guadalupe Hidalgo was signed. During Metro construction, the remains of the adobe were rediscovered and in large part preserved. In *Bandido!*, the sheriff and his men stop here in the Cahuenga Pass to prepare to ambush and capture Vásquez. It was a good place to end my geographical exploration in honor of a playwright who continues to give voice to the stories of Mexican Americans and their history in Los Angeles and throughout California.

César E. Chávez Avenue is that road that's named after el King César with the grapes and the marches. In L.A., there's this funny thing with naming the streets, everybody's got to see their hero up there on a sign like it means something.

— Yxta Maya Murray,
What It Takes to Get to Vegas (1999)

10 HISTORY BOOKS TO READ

This short stack of books will provide historical background that's broad, deep, and completely entertaining.

➤ CITY OF QUARTZ: EXCAVATING THE FUTURE IN LOS ANGELES, Mike Davis (1990) • The core of MacArthur Fellow Davis's book is his PhD thesis, but don't let that deter you. It's dystopian to a fault, though still essential reading to understand the city.

➤ AN EMPIRE OF THEIR OWN: HOW THE JEWS INVENTED HOLLYWOOD, Neal Gabler (1988) • The American dream of a group of Jewish immigrants becomes the beginning of Hollywood and American cinema.

➤ GOLDEN DREAMS: CALIFORNIA IN AN AGE OF ABUNDANCE, Kevin Starr (2009) • California's postwar era is told through fact and narrative in a way that works for both academics and casual history buffs.

➤ THE HISTORY OF FORGETTING: LOS ANGELES AND THE ERASURE OF MEMORY, Norman Klein (2008) • This exceptionally creative history, which weaves fiction into fact, was first published in 1997 and updated by the author a decade later.

➤ THE KING AND QUEEN OF MALIBU: THE TRUE STORY OF THE BATTLE FOR PARADISE, David K. Randall (2016) • A love story, a highway, and a history that connect locals to the land.

➤ L.A. NOIR: THE STRUGGLE FOR THE SOUL OF AMERICA'S MOST SEDUCTIVE CITY, John Buntin (2010) • A hugely entertaining history of mobsters, movie stars, cops, and studio chiefs in L.A.'s boom times from the 1920s through the midcentury.

➤ LOS ANGELES: THE ARCHITECTURE OF FOUR ECOLOGIES, Reyner Banham (2009) • This newer edition has a foreword that puts this influential 1970s analysis of L.A. architecture into contemporary perspective.

➤ THE MIRAGE FACTORY: ILLUSION, IMAGINATION, AND THE INVENTION OF LOS ANGELES, Gary Krist (2018) • Krist masterfully weaves together stories of William Mulholland, D.W. Griffith, and Aimee Semple McPherson and shows how they profoundly affected L.A.'s growth and culture.

➤ SOUTHERN CALIFORNIA: AN ISLAND ON THE LAND, Carey McWilliams (1946) • This fascinating analysis of Southern California remains relevant many decades after its publication date.

➤ WILSHIRE BOULEVARD: GRAND CONCOURSE OF LOS ANGELES, Kevin Roderick & J. Eric Lynxwiler (2005) • An insightful narrative and 150 vintage photos bring to life the history of Wilshire Boulevard and L.A.'s development as an auto-dependent metropolis.

THE PARTICULAR SADNESS OF LOS ANGELES
AIMEE BENDER

IN AIMEE BENDER'S coming-of-age novel *The Particular Sadness of Lemon Cake* (2010), her protagonist, Rose, who has a semi-magical ability to taste sadness and other emotions in food, falls in love with a small French restaurant in Los Feliz on Vermont near Franklin. Conveniently, the long-running Figaro Bistrot sits right near where Bender placed the fictional La Lyonnaise. With vintage chandeliers, bistro tables lining the sidewalk, and an ever-present crowd enjoying the steak frites, salade lyonnaise, and people-watching, Figaro is thick with French charm.

On a sunny spring afternoon, Bender joined me there to discuss *Lemon Cake*, Los Angeles as a setting, and why its literary community matters to her.

Born and raised on L.A.'s westside, she grounded *Lemon Cake* in "the flatlands near Hollywood," a place, like so many others, that's "fifteen minutes from a variety of crisscrossing freeways." She explained her desire to connect the L.A. she encounters every day with the L.A. she portrayed in the novel. "I mapped out where I thought Rose's home would be," she said. "I walked around those neighborhoods so much that it felt really anchored in me. Most of what I wrote before that wasn't set in L.A., so it felt like an acknowledgment of wanting the city to really play a role in the story.

"There's something kind of freeing about grounding the writing in real streets, in things that are mappable," she continued. "Places come and go, of course. I needed La Lyonnaise to have a certain kind of quality and space, so I had to make it up. But it certainly *could* be here."

At the time of our conversation, Bender was working on a new novel that takes place in another L.A. neighborhood. "I feel like in previous books I've covered the parts of L.A. that I wanted to cover in the city proper, so I've been thinking about where else I could put someone," she said.

Photo by Mark Miller

"I'm not drawn to writing about the westside because I grew up there—it's too familiar."

Bender has lived in L.A. most of her life; she moved to Irvine for the UC Irvine MFA program in the '90s. "A community of writers had formed there, and a lot of them were staying local, either in Irvine, Long Beach, or L.A.," she said. "I didn't want to lose that. It felt so precious. I was curious to see what it would be like to live as an adult in the city that I'd grown up in as a kid in a more suburban way. We lived in the Santa Monica/Brentwood area, and there was only one place my sisters and I could walk to. Other than that, it was all houses and didn't feel urban. To encounter the city as a city became important to me."

It's hard to pinpoint, Bender said, exactly when she knew she was going to be a writer. "I was writing in college and after college, and then I decided to get an MFA, but I still wasn't sure I could declare it as something I wanted as a career because it felt so wobbly and uncertain. I just knew I wanted to spend some time with it. Once I was in the MFA program, I started taking it seriously, and I got a lot of work done on what would become *The Girl in the Flammable Skirt*

And I realized as I walked through the neighborhood how each house could contain a completely different reality. In a single block, there could be fifty separate worlds. Nobody ever really knew what was going on just next door.

— JANET FITCH,
White Oleander (1999)

[her first book, a short-story collection]. That took what felt like a mirage and brought it into sharper focus."

Becoming part of a university literary community also helped Bender focus on her writing. And then, after her time at Irvine, her connection to the larger community of writers grew stronger. "When my first book was in galleys, I sent it out to look for teaching jobs," she said. "I ended up teaching at UCLA and Caltech and USC, and each had literary communities. I met a lot of people in each of those places. I was going to all the bookstores and to readings and meeting people there, and then there was the *Santa Monica Review*…. Dots on a map began to appear. It's been over twenty years, and most of the same people are still in town. Now I feel like I have deep roots in that world."

Los Angeles, she believes, has a particularly strong literary community. "It's not the film or TV business, so there's a natural underdog quality to the writing world," she said. "From the beginning, I found everyone to be really nice and interested in what's going on. We've all valued this thing that feels a little bit like an island out at sea."

Bender has continued to teach as she writes; she's currently a professor of creative writing at USC. Teaching has enriched her L.A. community because it's afforded her the opportunity to mentor young writers. "It's really fun to learn alongside them and from them," she said. "This semester, for example, I had a small-enough class that we had time in the semester to go to Skylight for a reading that Unnamed Press did for two of their authors. There was wine and cheese, a solid crowd, a lot of excitement—my students were all floored. They wrote reports saying things like, 'I never knew this was here,' and 'I feel bad I've never been to a reading before,' and 'I'm going to come again.'"

DO-GOOD BOOK PEOPLE

These nonprofits, educators, and just plain book lovers do so much to strengthen L.A.'s literacy and literature, and the city is grateful.

➤ **826 LA ECHO PARK & MAR VISTA** • L.A. is blessed with two locations for this vibrant national nonprofit, founded by author Dave Eggers in San Francisco with a mission to improve kids' literacy and inspire them to write. In venues hidden behind faux retail stores called the Time Travel Mart, 826 offers tutoring, workshops, and field trips; there's also an in-school program for those who can't get to the centers. Its annual fundraisers often draw a who's who of literary L.A.

➤ **BEYOND BAROQUE** • A literary and arts center in the former Venice City Hall building, it runs free youth programs, readings, and workshops for adults in poetry, fiction, and screenwriting, among other bookish events. The bookstore is stocked with works by independent creators, diverse voices, and local talent.

Behind the Time Travel Mart in Mar Vista is a lively space where kids revel in reading and writing.

➤ **BOOKSWELL** • The group connects L.A.'s readers and writers, making the local literary scene easy to navigate with a podcast, a free events calendar, and more.

➤ **COMMUNITY LITERATURE INITIATIVE** • This nonprofit teaches written and performance poetry and runs a writers-in-the-schools program. Affiliated with World Stage Press, CLI offers its signature class at USC, teaching writers how to create publishable manuscripts and connecting them with presses.

➤ **CREATING CONVERSATIONS** • Based in Redondo Beach, Creating Conversations organizes and runs author and literary events throughout Southern California for nonprofits, community luncheons, schools, libraries, and more.

➤ **GET LIT** • Get Lit empowers youth through literacy, with curriculum for poetry and performance used by more than 100 schools. With fellowships, classes, camps, and more, it has many ways to get involved.

➤ **LAMBDA LITERARY FOUNDATION** • With retreats, fellowships, awards, a writers-in-schools program, the annual LitFest, and more, Lambda elevates the voices of LGBTQ writers.

➤ **LIBRARY FOUNDATION OF LOS ANGELES** • The foundation has been dealing with controversy since its long-standing and respected Aloud event program was significantly changed, and many L.A. writers have canceled their memberships; time will tell if LFLA will recover.

➤ **LIBROS SCHMIBROS LENDING LIBRARY** • Based in Boyle Heights, Libros Schmibros provides low-cost and no-cost books to neighbors in Boyle Heights and East L.A. The nonprofit relies on book donations and grant support.

➤ **LITERATURE FOR LIFE** • This free curriculum for L.A.-area teachers, developed by the Light Bringer Project (also known for running both LitFest Pasadena and the Doo Dah Parade), brings together students, writers, illustrators, and educators.

➤ **LOS ANGELES POET SOCIETY** • LAPS hosts art and poetry showcases, facilitates youth and senior outreach, and runs a "womyn's writing circle," among other efforts.

➤ **LOS ANGELES REVIEW OF BOOKS** • LARB delivers everything from civic and public arts programs and literary events to a book-publishing division and a robust magazine and quarterly journal of interviews, reviews, essays, and more to Los Angeles readers interested in culture, the arts, and literature.

➤ **MICHAEL SILVERBLATT, KCRW** • The host of Bookworm, the beloved show on KCRW-FM (NPR), Silverblatt hosts authors every week in engaged and informed conversations about literature.

➤ **PASADENA LITERARY ALLIANCE** • The PLA fundraises for nonprofit literary programs, advocates for the literary arts, sponsors the hugely popular annual Pasadena Festival of Women Authors, and runs the author series called Open Book.

Libros Schmibros is part lending library, part used bookstore, and part community center.

➤ **PEN AMERICA** • PEN America is dedicated to defending and promoting free expression and literary excellence. Its initiatives include the Emerging Voices Fellowship, PEN in the Community, and the Los Angeles Literary Awards. Besides its public events, it works with imprisoned writers, students, multilingual writers, and others.

➤ **SAY WORD** • Say Word fosters literacy and creativity in young people through residencies, workshops, and an in-school program.

➤ **STREET POETS** • Street Poets works with at-risk and incarcerated youth via workshops, mentorship, reading series, open mics, organic gardening, and more.

➤ SIEL JU • A novelist who has a free digital guide to everything bookish in L.A., plus a worthwhile newsletter.

➤ WOMEN WHO SUBMIT • Through workshops and submission parties for women and nonbinary writers, WWS makes the writing and publishing process more accessible.

➤ WOMEN'S CENTER FOR CREATIVE WORK • A feminist creative community that hosts artists-in-residence, after-school programs, a community garden, a workspace, a library, and so much more.

➤ WOMEN'S NATIONAL BOOK ASSOCIATION LOS ANGELES • With a summer literacy program, writing critique groups, potlucks, an annual conference, and author events, L.A.'s branch of the WNBA (books, not basketball!) fosters literary community for writers of all genres.

➤ WRITEGIRL • WriteGirl pairs teenage girls with successful, professional women writers, who serve as mentors and lead workshops. It regularly publishes anthologies of the girls' work to amplify young voices.

This land deserves something better, in the way of inhabitants, than the swamis, the realtors, the motion-picture tycoons, the fakirs, the fat widows, the nondescript clerks, the bewildered ex-farmers, the corrupt pension-plan schemers, the tight-fisted "empire builders," and all the other curious migratory creatures who have flocked here from the far corners of the earth. For this strip of coast, this tiny region, seems to be looking westward across the Pacific, waiting for the future that one can somehow sense, and feel, and see. Here America will build its great city of the Pacific, the most fantastic city in the world.

— CAREY MCWILLIAMS, *Southern California: An Island on the Land* (1946)

HUNGRY FOR LOS ANGELES
M.F.K. FISHER &
JONATHAN GOLD

TWO OF THE GREATEST FOOD WRITERS in the English language are M.F.K. Fisher (1908–1992) and Jonathan Gold (1960–2018), both of whom hailed from the L.A. area. Fisher grew up in Whittier, which in the early 1900s was a distant Quaker suburb of L.A. but today is just another part of the megalopolis. Gold grew up in 1960s Los Angeles in a Beverlywood-adjacent area he called "Baja Beverly Hills," settling later in Pasadena with his wife, editor Laurie Ochoa, and their children.

Starting in the late 1930s, Mary Frances Kennedy Fisher wrote about food in a lush, sensual way that no American writer ever had. In twenty-seven books, she described her childhood in Whittier (*Among Friends*); her life as a young woman with first husband Al Fisher in Dijon, France, where she became enraptured with food (*The Gastronomical Me*); her years back in the L.A. area (Eagle Rock, Laguna, and beyond) during the Depression; and the decades after that in France and California. In her foreword to a recent edition of *The Gastronomical Me*, Ruth Reichl wrote, "She was the first to write about food as a way of understanding the world, and with *The Gastronomical Me* she virtually invented the food memoir. And long before food and food studies became fashionable, she was insisting that we would all be better if we studied our own hungers."

In *As They Were*, a collection of memoir essays, Fisher shared a happy childhood memory of Los Angeles: "Sometimes people can know two palaces before Lady Luck calls it quits... The lesser of the two palaces was the Pig'n Whistle, a stylish ice cream parlor... on Broadway, near the Orpheum Theatre, I think, convenient to the Pacific Electric Depot, where we could catch the Red Car back to Whittier after refreshment and revival." (The greater of the two palaces for young Mary Frances was the grand Riverside Mission Inn.)

Sharing food with another human being is an intimate act that should not be indulged in lightly.

— M.F.K. Fisher, *An Alphabet for Gourmets* (1949)

A trained musician, Gold first found his writing voice while covering music for the *LA Weekly*, before falling in love with the gastronomical life of the city. Over time, the city's food lovers became obsessed with his restaurant reviews, which were conversational, funny, intently observational cultural treatises as much as they were accounts of dishes eaten—which is why his one and only book, the restaurant guide *Counter Intelligence*, remains so eminently readable two decades after publication. His annual list of his 101 favorite restaurants would send foodies stampeding across the city in search of a great meal.

Gold is perhaps most admired for the way he championed small, often immigrant-run mom-and-pop restaurants, typically transforming the lives of their owners with his reviews. It was the power of his prose that made those reviews so influential (and that won him a Pulitzer Prize). He began his review of Matsuhisa, for example, this way:

> I have noted the hush that fell on a roomful of gangsta rappers when Quincy Jones walks into the studio, and seen a roomful of fiction writers breathe the words of a Raymond Carver story as the emphysematic author struggled through a reading late in his life... But I have never, I think, seen the unmuted awe that Nobu Matsuhisa commands when he strides through the Japanese fish wholesalers just east of downtown Los Angeles.

Even Gold's few years away in New York did not dim his hometown's love for him, nor his love for his hometown. To understand the impact of Jonathan Gold, and to understand L.A.'s food culture, do yourself a favor and watch the superb documentary about him, *City of Gold*.

The greatest Los Angeles cooking, real Los Angeles cooking, has first a sense of wonder about it, and only then a sense of place, because the place it has a sense of is likely to be somewhere else entirely. Los Angeles is, after all, where certain parts of town have stood in for Connecticut or Indiana so often on TV that they look more authentic than the real thing; where neighborhoods are called Little India, Little Tokyo, Little Central America, and Koreatown; where a typical residential block might include a couple of Spanish haciendas, a Tudor mansion, two thatched Cotswold cottages, a Palladian villa, and a cream puff of an imitation Loire château.

Image by Goro Toshina from the film City of Gold; courtesy Sundance Selects

— JONATHAN GOLD, *Counter Intelligence* (2000)

MUST-HAVE GUIDEBOOKS

From the mainstream to the quirky, here's a range of titles representing explorations of the city for myriad interests.

➤ THE 500 HIDDEN SECRETS OF LOS ANGELES, Andrea Richards (2019) • Of the many general guidebooks to the city, this is the current champ, featuring the five best of everything, from Rat Pack restaurants to places to buy an Oscars dress.

➤ AN ARCHITECTURAL GUIDEBOOK TO LOS ANGELES, Robert Winter, David Gebhard & Robert Inman (2018) • Now in its sixth edition, this is a must-read for any architecture buff.

➤ COUNTER INTELLIGENCE: WHERE TO EAT IN THE REAL LOS ANGELES, Jonathan Gold (2000) • As much an incisive cultural exploration as it is an entertaining restaurant guidebook; some of the restaurants are long gone, but the reviews make for great reading anyway.

➤ HOMETOWN PASADENA, Colleen Dunn Bates (2018) • Culture, history, art, interviews, features, advice, and inspiration about this exceptional L.A. satellite city.

➤ L.A. BIZARRO: THE ALL-NEW INSIDER'S GUIDE TO THE OBSCURE, THE ABSURD, AND THE PERVERSE IN LOS ANGELES, Anthony Lovett & Matt Maranian (2009) • The essential guide to L.A. things, ranging from the mildly quirky to the outright freakish.

➤ LOS ANGELES ATTRACTIONS, Borislav Stanic (2008) • It's rather dated, but it remains the most informed, best-organized general guide to the city.

➤ SECRET STAIRS: A WALKING GUIDE TO THE HISTORIC STAIRCASES OF LOS ANGELES, Charles Fleming (2010) • A simple guidebook to the hidden public stairs in L.A.; it became a surprise bestseller and has inspired countless urban explorers.

➤ THIS IS (NOT) L.A., Jen Bilik (2018) • With verve and wit, this visually dynamic book debunks many myths about L.A.

CATALINA IN THE DISTANCE
LISKA JACOBS

LISKA JACOBS'S ACCLAIMED DEBUT NOVEL, *Catalina*, details a young woman's unraveling after she leaves her life in New York to return to the city of her young womanhood, Los Angeles. Along with the titular location, Catalina Island, Elsa's misadventures with drugs, drinking, and morally questionable behavior also take her to the Fairmont Miramar Hotel in Santa Monica.

With bungalows dating to 1921 fronting a more modern tower hotel, the Miramar fairly screams "California," from its gardens to its palm-tree-framed pool to its location across the street from ocean-overlook Palisades Park. From the restaurant, the fictional Elsa Fisher watches her fellow guests in the pool, so Jacobs and I met in the same spot, watching the poolside parade while we talked.

"The Miramar was on my radar because my dad grew up nearby in Brentwood, and he used to tell me stories about it from when he was young," she said. "His parents used to party at the Chateau Marmont, but that's not where the cool kids partied in his day—they went to the Miramar." She continued, "I like the idea of there being an old glamour to this place that doesn't really translate to today. No one really thinks about the Miramar as somewhere to go to get drunk."

Jacobs comes from a long line of Angelenos, which is why it was so important to her to write well about her city. "My parents were born here, my father's parents were born here, and their parents were born here," she said. "That's why I really felt the need to represent Los Angeles accurately." Like Elsa, who left what seemed

like a dream job at MoMA in New York to return to L.A., Jacobs left what she thought was a dream job at the Getty Research Institute to become a writer, drafting *Catalina* while taking writing classes through UCLA Extension, then getting an MFA at UC Riverside while working at the Last Bookstore.

Photo by Jordan Bryant

In this city where she is so rooted, Jacobs draws inspiration. "I love drinking and hanging out in hotels in Los Angeles," she said. "Mostly because they tend to be the only places that remain constant. I mean, until recently, you could still have a mai tai at Trader Vic's in the Beverly Hilton. [After six decades, the infamous outpost closed in 2017.] But the hotel still stays. You can still walk through the same lobby that's always been there and watch people filter through. Hanging out in hotels gives me a sense of how outsiders view L.A., and it helps me look at the city with fresh eyes."

Her interest in impermanence is reflected in her fiction. Jacobs spoke, for example, about how the city changes by the time Elsa returns just a few years later, and she addressed the changes in a scene set at the Santa Monica Pier. "I thought it was important that it wasn't the same pier that she grew up with," Jacobs said. "It wasn't even the same Ferris wheel—that was destroyed in a storm in the '90s. I wanted to create a feeling of how, especially on the West Coast, everything is constantly being demolished and new things are being built." She added, "We don't really protect our landmarks in L.A. I mean, the thing we're most known for is midcentury modernism—which was only sixty years ago.

"I wouldn't leave L.A. if the whole place tipped over into the ocean," Mary declared. And indeed, she only left Los Angeles on urgent business. She was too tough and too fragile for anyplace else.

— Eve Babitz, *Slow Days, Fast Company* (1977)

"I think West Coast people have an inferiority complex, and Angelenos even feel that way toward our San Francisco neighbors," she said. "We can't help it. It's because we just don't have the layers of history." That makes L.A., she thinks, quite a useful setting for a writer. "You're able to put a lot of stories against it. You're able to really see how human beings act now, because L.A. is very much a contemporary city. Not modern—we don't have a great train system or public transportation or anything like that—but because we're so new, how human beings act is at the forefront of everything."

Jacobs has found tremendous community as a writer in Los Angeles. "The literary community here is so healthy and welcoming and large and eager for new talent," she said. "I used to feel terrified that there wasn't enough pie for everybody, but as I went to UCLA and UCR and worked at the bookstore, I came to learn that that's not the case. No one is rooting against you here, which sounds bizarre—I know how cutthroat the entertainment business is. But the literary community is very, very welcoming."

Jacobs went to college on the East Coast but transferred to UCLA mid-semester because of the enduring pull of home. She finds L.A. exceptionally welcoming too. "It doesn't matter if you're not from here—we welcome everybody," she said. "That's what keeps a community vibrant. We don't shut doors to people who come here and fall in love with the place. We don't even shut the door if you don't love it! If you write a whole diatribe about how much you hate L.A. and it's written well, I promise people will show up to the reading.

"It's amazing. I wouldn't want to live anywhere else."

The challenge and the glory of Los Angeles is that it changes so fast that it defies definition. You can't really chronicle L.A., except maybe in a tweet. L.A. was built in one hour, on a very hot Friday afternoon.

— CHRIS ERSKINE, *Daditude* (2018)

BEHOLD THE LORE OF L.A. AUTHORS!

By Mike Sonksen

I grew up going to bookstores across Los Angeles. From the early 1980s, I remember my dad driving us to the Bodhi Tree on Melrose, Acres of Books in Long Beach, and many other bookstores now long gone. By the time I started UCLA in 1992, I was driving my friends to Midnight Special in Santa Monica, Chatterton's (which became Skylight Books) in Los Feliz, Hennessey & Ingalls in Santa Monica, Book Soup on Sunset, Beyond Baroque in Venice, Eso Won Books when it was on La Brea, and the little bookstore on Franklin in Hollywood. Buying books was a habit I acquired early, and my genres of choice are nonfiction and poetry. What follows are a few of my favorites—there are countless more, but these will provide a great introduction to the firmament of Los Angeles letters. Behold the lore of L.A. authors!

5 NONFICTION TITLES

➤ **POPULAR CULTURE IN THE AGE OF WHITE FLIGHT** • Eric Avila
Spotlighting Disneyland, Dodger Stadium, the rise of the freeway system, and film genres like noir and science fiction, Eric Avila masterfully shows how popular culture reflected the political and social changes that happened in Los Angeles in the two decades following World War II. This landmark book demonstrates how "the reconfiguration of the American city initiated the decline of both the new mass culture and its urban context and inaugurated a new paradigm of race and space."

➤ **CENTRAL AVENUE SOUNDS** • Edited by Clora Bryant, Steve Isoardi & others
This important work collects oral histories on the historic Central Avenue jazz district that existed in L.A. from the 1920s into the early 1960s. Featuring memories and insights from luminaries who were there, like Clora Bryant, Buddy Collette, Jack Kelson, Horace Tapscott, and Gerald Wilson, this 1998 book kick-started a renewed interest in Central Avenue, whose history at that point had been largely forgotten.

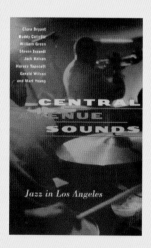

➤ **ECOLOGY OF FEAR** • Mike Davis
The predecessor of this book, 1990's *City of Quartz*, is often lauded as the book that really launched Los Angeles studies. This is true, but *Ecology of Fear* is just as good.

Nobody writes better about fire and the chaparral landscapes in L.A. than Davis. Furthermore, his chapters "The Literary Destruction of Los Angeles," "How Eden Lost Its Garden," and "Beyond Blade Runner" are groundbreaking passages that paved the way for dozens of scholars.

➤ **AFTER/IMAGE: LOS ANGELES OUTSIDE THE FRAME** • Lynell George
Lynell George's essays and photographs, published by L.A.'s Angel City Press, examine and explicate Los Angeles with an uncanny verisimilitude. Rooted in personal experience, she catalogs the changing landscape, delving deeply into the city's shifting districts and ever-evolving zeitgeist coming to rise because of these shifts. A lifetime of covering her hometown is distilled into eleven meticulous essays complemented perfectly by her own poignant, original photography.

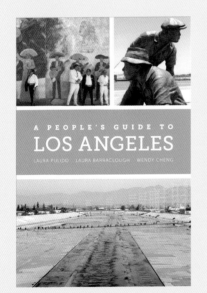

8 MORE NONFICTION TITLES TO LOOK FOR

1. Whitewashed Adobe • William Deverell
2. Counter Intelligence: Where to Eat in the Real Los Angeles • Jonathan Gold
3. The Power of Place • Dolores Hayden
4. The Tide Was Always High (L.A. musical history) • edited by Josh Kun
5. Latinx Writing Los Angeles • edited by Ignacio López-Calvo and Victor Valle
6. Piecing Together Los Angeles • Esther McCoy
7. Southern California: An Island on the Land • Carey McWilliams
8. Becoming Mexican American • George J. Sánchez

➤ **A PEOPLE'S GUIDE TO LOS ANGELES** • Edited by Laura Pulido, Laura R. Barraclough & Wendy Cheng
Subverting the typical L.A. guidebook, *A People's Guide* contains more than 300 pages of sites, stories, and maps "where struggles related to class, race, gender, sexuality, and the environment have occurred." It maps 115 places/stories across the basin, including familiar ones like the L.A. Black Panthers, Chavez Ravine, and Self-Help Graphics, but the work's true magic is its celebration of such lesser-known sites as Biddy Mason Park, Kashu Realty, Cambodiatown, the Southern California Research Library, and the Studio for Southern California History.

5 POETRY TITLES

➤ **COILED SERPENT** • Edited by Neelanjana Banerjee, Daniel A. Olivas & Ruben J. Rodriguez

Published by L.A.'s own Tía Chucha, this collection is undoubtedly the largest anthology of L.A. poetry ever published, with works from such well-known, seasoned scribes as Wanda Coleman, Kamau Daáood, Michael C. Ford, California State Poet Laureate Dana Gioia, Peter J. Harris, Rubén Martinez, S. Pearl Sharp, Amy Uyematsu, and Terry Wolverton and such up-and-coming bards as Xochitl-Julisa Bermejo, F. Douglas Brown, Jessica Ceballos, Chiwan Choi, Francisco Escamilla, William Gonzalez, Douglas Kearney, traci kato-kiriyama, Teka Lark, Karineh Mahdessian, Jeffrey Martin, Luivette Resto, and Vickie Vértiz.

➤ **IMAGOES** • By Wanda Coleman

The author of nearly twenty books, Wanda Coleman was dubbed L.A.'s unofficial poet laureate for many years and she has written dozens of iconic Los Angeles poems. *Imagoes* was her second book and the one she considered her breakout title. Among the 104 poems in the collection, pieces like "I Live for My Car," "Flight of the California Condor," and "Prisoner of Los Angeles" capture the City of Angels as well as any poems ever written. In the latter poem she writes:

> so this is it, i say to the enigma in the mirror
> this is your lot/assignment/relegation
> this is your city
>
> i find my way to the picture window
> my eyes capture the purple reach of hollywood's hills
> the gold eye of sun mounting the east
> the gray anguished arms of avenue
>
> i will never leave here

➤ **THE LANGUAGE OF SAXOPHONES** • By Kamau Daáood

Cofounder of the seminal Leimert Park performance space called the World Stage, Kamau Daáood has been an L.A. poet since the late 1960s and was originally the youngest member of the Watts Writers Workshop. His City

Lights book *The Language of Saxophones* collects nearly forty years of his poetry, including odes to his wife and his mother, and to Billie Holiday, John Coltrane, Billy Higgins, Horace Tapscott, and Charlie Parker, among many others. Daáood is also incredible live.

➤ CITY OF THE FUTURE • Sesshu Foster
Sesshu Foster is one of the most influential Angeleno poets of the last generation. His 1996 book, *City Terrace Field Manual*, was groundbreaking for its hybrid poetics. *City of the Future*, published by L.A.'s Kaya Press, continues his legacy of mapping the real Los Angeles and resisting the "apartheid imagination." This book bends such genres as documentary and poetry with surrealism and the elegiac. Born to a Japanese American mother and Caucasian father, Foster is often assumed to be Chicano because he's spent so many years in the Latinx arts community and has lived almost all his life in East Los Angeles.

8 MORE POETRY TITLES TO LOOK FOR

1. Psychosis in the Produce Department • Laurel Ann Bogen
2. Voices from Leimert Park Redux: Los Angeles Poetry Anthology • edited by Shonda Buchanan
3. Women Under the Influence • Michael C. Ford
4. A Wild Surmise: New & Selected Poems & Recordings • Eloise Klein Healy
5. Dear Oxygen: New & Selected Poems 1966–2011 • Lewis MacAdams
6. Urban Tumbleweed • Harryette Mullen
7. The Concrete River • Luis J. Rodriguez
8. 30 Miles from J-Town • Amy Uyematsu

➤ WIDE AWAKE: POETS OF LOS ANGELES AND BEYOND • Edited by Suzanne Lummis
This collection features the work of more than 112 L.A. poets. In her introduction, Lummis writes, "These poems endorse neither the dream nor the nightmare vision of Los Angeles. Instead they wander through absurdity, pathos, comedy, anguish, irony, and tenderness. And through NELA, NoHo, West L.A., Venice West, Malibu, Hollywood, East Hollywood, Downtown, K-Town, J-Town, East Los, and Leimert Park they wander, usually with a purpose." Each poem is a separate story, and the 200-plus poems follow a loose geographic narrative, but most of all they capture the wide-ranging spirit of the city.

Mike Sonksen, aka Mike the Poet, is a third-generation Angeleno, a poet, a literary historian, a faculty member at Southwest College and Woodbury, a columnist for KCET, and an organizer of community readings and literary events. Follow him on aliveinlosangeles.com.

Is it the sunshine or catastrophes?
Flash floods or the traffic?

Something about Los Angeles
makes music, makes magic.
The muse of Los Angeles
makes artists get active.
Behold the lore of L.A. authors!

Who's rocking the populace
in the postmodern metropolis?
L.A. Authors

— MIKE SONKSEN,
from *Letters to My City* (2019)

THE PLAYER PLAYS AGAIN
MICHAEL TOLKIN

MICHAEL TOLKIN WROTE one of the great novels about the film industry, 1988's *The Player*, a story about the unraveling of a studio executive that he later adapted into a screenplay for the 1992 Robert Altman film. Eager to talk about literature and the film industry and how they intersect, I asked him to meet me at the Grill on the Alley in Beverly Hills, where his protagonist from *The Player* has a pitch meeting with a writer.

"The wood-paneled room, with comfortable booths and small tables, was supposed to remind you of old Hollywood," wrote Tolkin of the Grill in *The Player*, and it remains a place where deals happen. So it was the perfect setting to talk about the fictional deals depicted in *The Player*, as well as his career as a novelist and screenwriter.

Tolkin's father was a television writer in New York who moved his family to L.A. for his work. Tolkin returned east for college, and it didn't take him long to follow in his father's writing footsteps. "The first thing I wrote was a screenplay when I was between colleges," he said. "It was a sequel to *Two-Lane Blacktop*, and it was about Cabazon, a town that was bypassed when the freeway came through. It was angry and wild. I haven't read it in a long time." After college, he worked as a freelance journalist in New York for *The Village Voice* and other publications, but after realizing that he really wasn't a reporter at heart, he moved home to L.A. to pursue more creative writing.

"Through a connection, I got a job working on a television series based on *Animal House* that didn't last, but I got an introduction to Hollywood and filmmaking," he said. "Then I had a dry patch, and I wasn't sure if I was really a writer." He used his down time to read everything by Patricia Highsmith and James M. Cain, who, he said, "became my literary mother and father, and that's when I came up with the idea for *The Player*. It was really a merger of my sense

Photo by Jacek Laskus

Los Angeles is a large city-like area surrounding the Beverly Hills Hotel.

— FRAN LEBOWITZ, *Social Studies* (1981)

of the two of them." He started writing the novel but kept a low profile about it. "A friend was working on a novel and was very public about it. Everyone knew what chapter he was on and all the difficulties he was having, and I thought, 'He's a real writer and I don't know what I am.' So in the years I was working on *The Player*, only four people knew what I was doing. During that time, I also wrote a movie, *Gleaming the Cube*, and instead of using the money to buy a car, I used it to buy the time to finish the novel."

Tolkin's time in Hollywood had a huge impact on writing *The Player*. "It was what I knew," he said. "My father was a writer and my mother was a studio lawyer. They were educated and into culture, so the talk at the dinner table was about music, literature, and art—and Hollywood." It therefore seemed perfectly reasonable to start adapting the novel as a screenplay. "A famous producer named David Brown read the manuscript and called me, said he had no money to option it but he'd make me a partner," Tolkin said. "He encouraged me to write the script, and I did, and then we took it around. People were afraid of a Hollywood movie, but David didn't give up. When Robert Altman changed agencies, they gave him my script, and after that it was a pretty smooth process."

Tolkin's most recent book, *NK3*, is a dystopian novel about Los Angeles. In it, memories and the skills that go with them have been erased, leaving people either completely incapable of higher mental functions or with only a playacting understanding of how to do important work, like surgery. It wasn't a stretch for him to create a dark vision of his city in the future because, he said, "L.A. is a dystopia." He worked particularly hard on getting the locations right.

"I was really happy naming the towns and tried to be geographically correct. That mattered a lot to me. In New York fiction, when they talk about the Upper West Side, everyone knows where that is, but nobody knows where Alhambra is in literature. I wanted to have fun with writing Covina."

How he gets his ideas, and whether they take form as a novel or script, remains unclear even to him. "My books have come to me in a mystical way—they just appeared," Tolkin said. "I discovered *NK3* as I was thinking about other ideas. It's almost as though I'm two different people, a novelist and a screenwriter. With *Among the Dead*, it started out as a possible movie, but as I did research, I realized it was a book. If the idea comes with a lot of complexity and character, then it feels better as a book. It's a mysterious process, and somehow it gets sorted out."

Tolkin continues to write about L.A. because, he said, "it's almost unexplored territory." As for the writing world, he differs from his peers who find L.A.'s community strong. "There are a lot of good writers, but there isn't really a literary society," he said. "The *L.A. Times* doesn't take care of its own literary world and doesn't make a point of creating a sense that there's a literary universe here, which is a mistake because it means that writers are working in certain isolation from each other. They're all responding to the city, the same attributes, but from a different point of view."

Our conversation concluded with his observations about the difference between books by L.A. authors and movies and TV shows filmed in L.A. "So many movie stories have been set here arbitrarily," he said. "They're shot here, but they're not really *about* L.A.—the city is just a location. That opens the opportunity for novelists to explore what people have seen for years but don't really know."

To everyone from back home, L.A. was one big city. They didn't know L.A. was a thousand little towns, entire worlds re-created in arroyos and strawberry fields and hillsides.

— SUSAN STRAIGHT,
"The Golden Gopher"
in *Los Angeles Noir* (1997)

WRITERS ON DRIVING

People are afraid to merge on freeways in Los Angeles. This is the first thing I hear when I come back to the city. Blair picks me up from LAX and mutters this under her breath as she drives up the onramp. She says, "People are afraid to merge on freeways in Los Angeles." Though that sentence shouldn't bother me, it stays in my mind for an uncomfortably long time. Nothing else seems to matter.

— Bret Easton Ellis, *Less Than Zero* (1985)

A good part of any day in Los Angeles is spent driving, alone, through streets devoid of meaning to the driver, which is one reason the place exhilarates some people, and floods others with an amorphous unease. There is about these hours spent in transit a seductive unconnectedness.

— Joan Didion, *After Henry* (1992)

In Southern California, you don't go down to a cafe and drink a lot of coffee and talk about intellectual concepts the way you might in Prague. You get in the car, drive for an hour, have a long, leisurely lunch in a beautiful yard, and get the same material covered. There's a kind of daytime quality to a lot of literary life here—not a suburban quality, but a domestic one.

— Carolyn See, quoted in *Sidewalking* by David L. Ulin

An afternoon drive from Los Angeles will take you up into the high mountains, where eagles circle above the forests and the cold blue lakes, or out over the Mojave Desert, with its weird vegetation and immense vistas. Not very far away are Death Valley, and Yosemite, and Sequoia Forest with its giant trees, which were growing long before the Parthenon was built; they are the oldest living things in the world. One should visit such places often, and be conscious, in the midst of the city, of their surrounding presence. For this is the real nature of California and the secret of its fascination; this untamed, undomesticated, aloof, prehistoric landscape which relentlessly reminds the traveler of his human condition and the circumstances of his tenure upon the earth.

— CHRISTOPHER ISHERWOOD, *Exhumations* (1966)

The rain continued through Monday morning and slowed Bosch's drive into Brentwood to a frustrating crawl. It wasn't heavy rain, but in Los Angeles any rain at all can paralyze the city. It was one of the mysteries Bosch could never fathom. A city largely defined by the automobile yet full of drivers unable to cope with even a mild inclemency.

— MICHAEL CONNELLY, *Angels Flight* (1998)

Anaheim is beautiful. Supremo freeway access in all directions. All that concrete crisscrossing in the air, north, south, east, and west, a compass rose.

— JIM GAVIN, *Middle Men* (2004)

MUST-READ L.A. FICTION

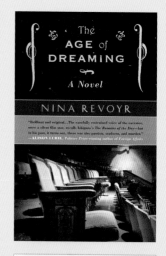

➤ **THE AGE OF DREAMING**, Nina Revoyr (2008) • The fictional memoir of an aging Japanese American silent movie star, set in 1920s and '60s Hollywood.

➤ **ASK THE DUST**, John Fante (1939) • Angry, ambitious young writer in 1930s downtown L.A. meets angrier waitress in one of L.A.'s most influential novels.

➤ **BAKED**, Mark Haskell Smith (2010) • A pacifist pot grower attempts to get revenge and recover his prize-winning product alongside a questionable cast of characters. Hilarity ensues.

➤ **THE BARBARIAN NURSERIES**, Héctor Tobar (2011) • An essential novel of Southern California life that explores the intersections of race, class, culture, and ambition through the novel's accidental protagonist, the somewhat prickly Mexican maid for a declining upper-class family.

➤ **BEIGE**, Cecil Castellucci (2007) • The city through the fresh eyes of a young, uptight newcomer who would rather be anywhere but with her unruly, punk rock dad; signature modern YA.

➤ **BETTER**, John O'Brien (2009) • Set in the party house of the wealthy and mysterious Double Felix, this novel portrays the residents' frivolous pursuits of pleasure and the complex ties of loyalty and humanity that bind them.

➤ **BLONDE**, Joyce Carol Oates (1999) • A masterful fictional retelling of the life of Marilyn Monroe that is perhaps as legendary as the icon herself.

➤ **THE COMEDY WRITER**, Peter Farrelly (1998) • Henry Halloran leaves his boring East Coast life and inexplicably finds success in 1990s Hollywood.

➤ **DAISY JONES & THE SIX**, Taylor Jenkins Reid (2019) • With the energy of Cameron Crowe's *Almost Famous*, *Daisy Jones* is written as an oral history of a fictitious celebrated band of 1970s L.A.

➤ **THE DAY OF THE LOCUST**, Nathanael West (1939) • Desperation, alienation, and an infamous angry mob converge in this Depression-era Hollywood classic.

➤ **THE DECENT PROPOSAL**, Kemper Donovan (2016) • This mystery/rom-com/drama/debut about contemporary Angelenos is described as Jane Austen in Los Angeles.

➤ **EVE'S HOLLYWOOD**, Eve Babitz (1974) • A collection of auto-fiction vignettes displaying Babitz's singular and sharp eye about the intersecting 1960s L.A. scenes, from rock 'n' roll to the corner taqueria.

➤ **GOLDEN DAYS**, Carolyn See (1986) • Quintessential L.A. literature about divorcée and single mom Edith Langley, spanning the '60s to the '80s, when nuclear annihilation turns the city into a wasteland.

➤ **HELEN OF PASADENA**, Lian Dolan (2010) • A romantic comedy that nails the private-school, old-money, country-club side of Pasadena culture.

➤ **HOLLYWOOD WIVES**, Jackie Collins (1983) • Decades before any real housewives graced our small screens, Collins's wives dazzled in this story of intersecting characters in the 1980s Hollywood of fame, fortune, and murder.

➤ **IF HE HOLLERS LET HIM GO**, Chester Himes (1945) • With power and wit, Himes addresses racism and segregation in 1940s L.A., issues the city still struggles with.

➤ **IN THE NOT QUITE DARK**, Dana Johnson (2016) • Set almost entirely in DTLA, this collection of short stories from award-winning Johnson reflects on history, family, race, and more.

➤ **LESS THAN ZERO**, Bret Easton Ellis (1985) • Ellis's first novel, written when he was an undergrad, is a tour de force through the intersection of early-'80s L.A. wealth, its drug culture, and the alienation of young people.

➤ **LOCAS**, Yxta Maya Murray (1997) • Two young Latinas in Echo Park cope with gang warfare, one by being angry and tough, the other by turning to prayer and the Church.

➤ **LOS ANGELES STORIES**, Ry Cooder (2011) • Cooder is almost as talented a writer as he is a guitar player, as evidenced by this collection of noirish stories set in the hardscrabble musician worlds of Chavez Ravine, Bunker Hill, and Venice.

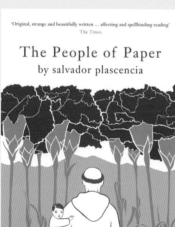

➤ **LOVE AND ROCKETS** series, Hernandez brothers: Gilbert, Jaime, and Mario (1982–present) • The beloved graphic series about the adventures of Maggie, her best friend Hopey, and their group of companions.

➤ **THE LOVE OF THE LAST TYCOON**, F. Scott Fitzgerald (1941) • AKA *The Last Tycoon*, this is Fitzgerald's unfinished final novel, about 1930s Hollywood.

➤ **THE LOVED ONE**, Evelyn Waugh (1948) • A dark, satirical comedy about British expats in L.A., Hollywood, and the over-the-top, Forest Lawn–style funeral business.

➤ **MIDDLE MEN**, Jim Gavin (2004) • Poignant, wryly funny stories about ordinary guys in and around Long Beach who are striving for middle-class success; some of them inspired Gavin's AMC series *Lodge 49*.

➤ **THE PEOPLE OF PAPER**, Salvador Plascencia (2005) • The setting is the real El Monte, but the story encompasses absurdism and magical realism, all to captivating effect.

➤ **THE PISCES**, Melissa Broder (2018) • A fabulist love story set in Venice about a woman in a love-addiction therapy group who becomes obsessed with a merman.

➤ **PLAY IT AS IT LAYS**, Joan Didion (1970) • With her singular and intense prose, Didion confronts the ennui of late-'60s American culture in this timeless L.A. masterpiece.

➤ **THE PLAYER**, Michael Tolkin (1988) • This classic satirical novel about Griffin Mill, a Hollywood executive in the late-'80s era of excess, went on to become an equally classic Robert Altman film.

➤ **THE POST OFFICE**, Charles Bukowski (1971) • A work of autofiction that follows Bukowski's alter-ego Henry Chinaski through his years of gambling, drinking, and womanizing while working on and off for the USPS in L.A.

➤ **RAMONA, Helen Hunt Jackson (1884)** • It's dated, and it reflects the assumptions of the era, but this hugely popular 1884 novel about a mixed-race orphan girl was groundbreaking for its time, luring many to SoCal and drawing attention to the mistreatment of Native Americans.

➤ **SHOOTING ELVIS, Robert Eversz (1996)** • A good-girl-gone-bad thriller set in late-1990s L.A.

➤ **SHOPGIRL, Steve Martin (2000)** • This delightful novella of modern love is filtered through Martin's witty and observant lens.

➤ **A SINGLE MAN, Christopher Isherwood (1964)** • His best-known work, taking place over twenty-four hours, is a meditative portrait of a middle-aged gay man coping with the sudden loss of his partner.

➤ **SUDDEN RAIN, Maritta Wolf (2005)** • Published posthumously and set in 1972, this novel examines the American dream through three generations of middle-class Angelenos.

➤ **THE SYMPATHIZER, Viet Thanh Nguyen (2015)** • A gorgeously written satirical modern tale of an erudite Vietnamese spy who ends up in L.A. after the fall of Saigon.

➤ **THIS BOOK WILL SAVE YOUR LIFE, A.M. Homes (2007)** • Middle-aged Richard has an existential crisis and begins to connect with those around him in this funny, surreal, L.A.-based novel.

➤ **THIS WICKED WORLD, Richard Lange (2009)** • Jimmy Boone, an ex-Marine, ex-con bartender, helps a buddy investigate the mysterious death of a young migrant worker on a bus in this neo-noir novel.

➤ **THE TORTILLA CURTAIN, T.C. Boyle (1995)** • Boyle's tragicomedy about immigration, poverty, racism, the middle class, and the environment should be required reading.

➤ **TROPIC OF ORANGE, Karen Tei Yamashita (1997)** • A wildly inventive hip hop/noir/magical realism/apocalyptic 1997 novel involving tainted oranges and the Harbor Freeway.

➤ **WEETZIE BAT, Francesca Lia Block (1989)** • Block's debut, now a YA institution, is a fabulist coming-of-age story set in and about L.A.; it's the first in a series of five, known collectively as *Dangerous Angels*.

➤ **WHAT MAKES SAMMY RUN?, Budd Schulman (1941)** • The rags-to-riches story of Sammy Glick, a 1940s Hollywood player who succeeds by any means (and was inspired by the author's father), by the screenwriter of *On the Waterfront*.

➤ **THE WHITE BOY SHUFFLE, Paul Beatty (1996)** • Beatty's debut is a bildungsroman about Gunnar Kaufman, a surfer turned messiah on L.A.'s westside.

➤ **WHITE OLEANDER, Janet Fitch (1999)** • A powerhouse mother-daughter novel about imprisoned poet Ingrid and her daughter, Astrid, who's trapped in L.A.'s foster-care system.

➤ **WOMAN NO. 17, Edan Lepucki (2017)** • High in the Hollywood Hills, life gets complicated for a mother, her nanny, and her teenage son in this darkly comic sophomore novel.

➤ **WONDER VALLEY, Ivy Pochoda (2017)** • An empathetic novel of interlocking stories centered on six L.A. misfits, each of whom yearn for redemption.

➤ **ZEROVILLE, Steve Erickson (2007)** • This darkly funny story follows film editor Vikar through the evolution of making movies (read: the demise of creative filmmaking) in Hollywood.

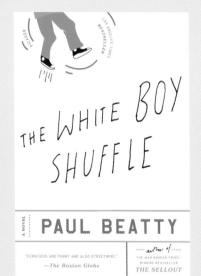
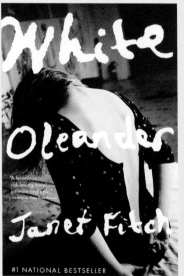

DOUBLE THE NOIR
JAMES M. CAIN

TRYING TO FIND James M. Cain's Los Angeles (and its environs) proved a harder task than I'd expected. He populated his noir novels—most notably *The Postman Always Rings Twice, Mildred Pierce,* and *Double Indemnity*—with seemingly specific L.A. locations, but often these are fictional or ephemeral.

In *The Postman Always Rings Twice,* for example, the fictional Twin Oaks Tavern is at the center of much of the action. The story in Cain's debut novel revolves around the tavern's owner, Nick Papadakis ("the Greek"), his younger wife, Cora, and Frank Chambers, a drifter they hire to help out at the place; Cora and Frank get involved and conspire to kill the Greek. The Twin Oaks is a roadhouse in the mountains above L.A., with a gas station and motel joining a restaurant to make Papadakis's little empire. Places like that were common in the 1930s and '40s but aren't today, so the few that are left are treasures. Newcomb's Ranch is one of them.

Newcomb's opened in what is now the Angeles National Forest in 1939, only a few years after Cain wrote *Postman.* It's a cheery, ranch-style wooden building set among pines, on winding Angeles Crest Highway about an hour north of Glendale, where the Papadakises would travel to do their shopping.

Newcomb's Ranch is a popular weekend destination for motorcyclists who stop for lunch after roaring up Angeles Crest Highway, and I enjoyed the drive up as much as they do. It's a gorgeous journey into the San Gabriel Mountains; if you go in winter, you might be fortunate enough to encounter trees flocked with snow and low-hanging clouds settling around the peaks.

When Chambers arrives at the Twin Oaks in the first chapter of *The Postman,* he orders "orange juice, corn flakes, fried eggs and bacon, enchilada, flapjacks, and coffee." I couldn't possibly manage all that, so I ordered fried eggs and coffee and absorbed the retro atmosphere that's not (other than the modern motorcycles and cars)

Newcomb's Ranch when the motorcyclists visit.

terribly different from what it was in the Twin Oaks era.

Breakfast complete, I headed back down the mountain to Glendale to explore the setting of *Mildred Pierce*, Cain's 1941 classic. Mildred finds success (for a while) during the Depression by opening a successful chicken-and-waffle restaurant in Glendale called Mildred's; she later adds branches in Beverly Hills and Laguna. They were, of course, fictional, and Glendale no longer has any 1930s-style chicken restaurants, although the older residential neighborhoods in this L.A. satellite city are filled with houses and apartments from the 1920s and '30s, giving me a feel for Mildred's era. And because the resting places of the dead don't get torn down for high-rises, one location remains from the novel: Glendale's Forest Lawn Cemetery, where Mildred's younger daughter, Ray, is buried after she dies of an infection. Had Ray Pierce been real, I would have searched for her grave. Instead I wandered around the rolling green hills studded with gravestones, thinking of Mildred's grief and the

Monty lay still, and smoked a long time. Then, in a queer, shaky voice he said: "I always said you'd make some guy a fine wife if you didn't live in Glendale."

"Are you asking me to marry you?"

"If you move to Pasadena, yes."

"You mean if I buy this house."

"No—it's about three times as much house as you need, and I don't insist on it. But I will not live in Glendale."

— JAMES M. CAIN, *Mildred Pierce* (1941)

mess she makes of her life as the novel progresses.

To complete a trifecta of locations from Cain's three major hard-boiled novels, I set out to get a feel for the L.A. in *Double Indemnity*. Many of its locations are sketched in loose terms—bungalows in the Los Feliz hills, Spanish mansions in the Hollywood Hills—but there are a few places and routes spelled out.

From Forest Lawn in Glendale, I headed west to Hollywood and up into the hills

Beachwood Market in the 1930s, when Cain was writing about the neighborhood.

via Beachwood Drive, one of my favorite streets in L.A. A pleasure to drive, it leads into the original Hollywoodland settlement of the early 1920s, where Cain himself lived and where he placed his *Double Indemnity* femme fatale, Phyllis Nirdlinger. Antihero Walter Huff is nudged into giving Lola, Phyllis's stepdaughter, Phyllis, and Lola's date, Mr. Sachetti, a ride down the hill to Hollywood and Vine. He first takes them to the drugstore on Beachwood, which I took to be the Beachwood Market, a neighborhood staple since 1933 that's well worth a stop.

Back then, Beachwood went south to Hollywood Boulevard, but the route was interrupted decades ago with the construction of the Hollywood Freeway. So instead of driving down to that famous intersection, I stayed in Beachwood Canyon and headed to 6301 Quebec Drive, Phyllis's house from Billy Wilder's masterful 1944 movie adaption. Not only does it look the same as it did in the movie, it even looks like how Cain describes it in the novel: "It was just a Spanish house, like all the rest of them in California, with white walls, red tile roof, and a patio out to one side. It was built cock-eyed. The garage was under the house, the first floor was over that, and the rest of it was spilled up the hill any way they could get it in. You climbed some stone steps to the front door, so I parked the car and went up there." Legend has it that Cain suggested this house for the movie location, which means this may have been the very house in which he pictured cold-blooded Phyllis when he was writing the story in the 1930s.

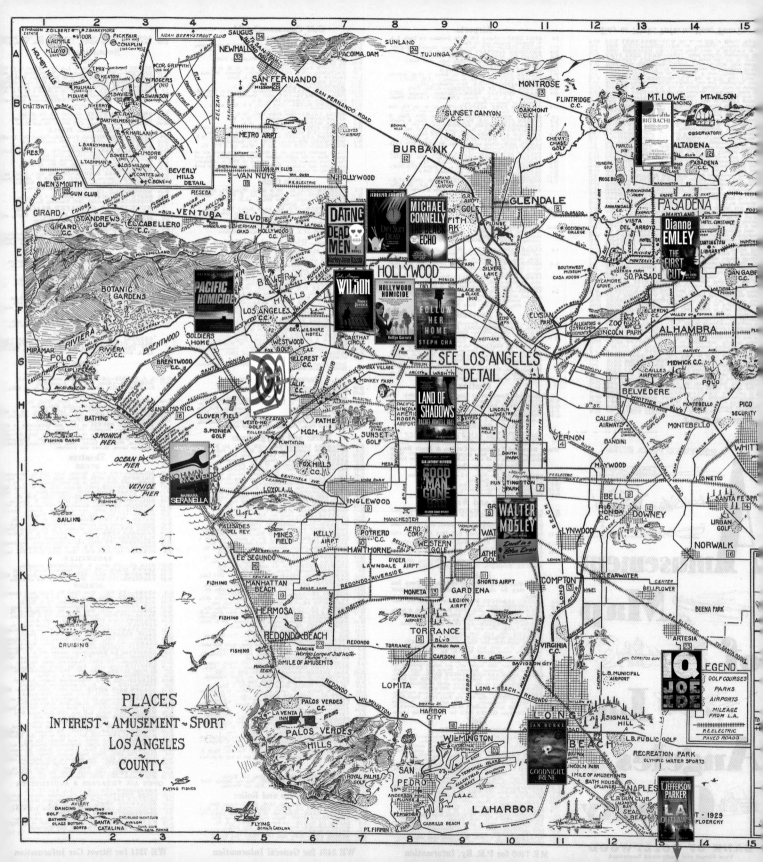

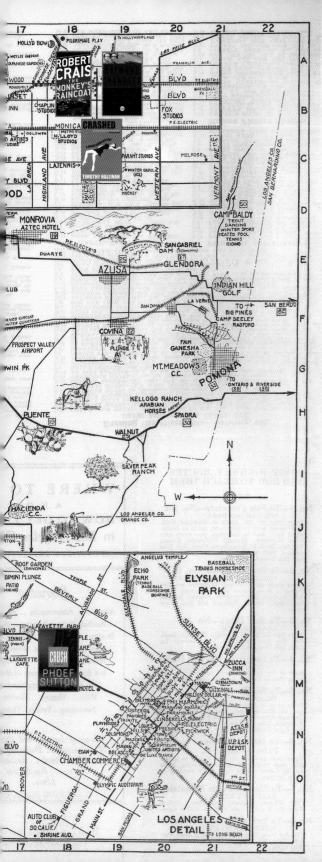

CRIME SOLVERS' MAP OF L.A.

Covers for books starring L.A.'s best fictional detectives pinpoint their home bases.

The Black Echo ➤ HARRY BOSCH

Crashed ➤ JUNIOR BENDER

Crush ➤ CRUSII

Dating Dead Men ➤ WOLLIE SHELLEY

Devil in a Blue Dress ➤ EASY RAWLINS

Dim Sum Dead ➤ MADELINE BEAN

The First Cut ➤ NAN VINING

Follow Her Home ➤ JUNIPER SONG

Good Man Gone Bad ➤ AARON GUNNER

Goodnight, Irene ➤ IRENE KELLY

Hollywood Homicide ➤ DAYNA ANDERSON

IQ ➤ ISAIAH QUINTABE

L.A. Outlaws ➤ CHARLIE HOOD

Land of Shadows ➤ ELOISE "LOU" NORTON

The Long Goodbye ➤ PHILIP MARLOWE

The Monkey's Raincoat ➤ ELVIS COLE

The Moving Target ➤ LEW ARCHER

No Human Involved ➤ MUNCH MANCINI

Pacific Homicide ➤ DAVIE RICHARDS

Simple Justice ➤ BENJAMIN JUSTICE

Summer of the Big Bachi ➤ MAS ARAI

FICTIONAL CRIME SOLVERS

Our favorite detectives, PIs, and amateur sleuths who are keeping L.A.'s bad guys at bay.

➤ **DAYNA ANDERSON**, created by Kellye Garrett • This actress turned private eye knows where the murderers are hiding behind the Hollywood glitz.

➤ **MAS ARAI**, created by Naomi Hirahara • A quiet, sometimes-cranky, always-intuitive retired gardener from Altadena who tends to come across dead bodies.

➤ **LEW ARCHER**, created by Ross Macdonald • One of the great hard-boiled private eyes, originally inspired by Philip Marlowe but evolving, over the course of the books, to be a little more sensitive.

➤ **MADELINE BEAN**, created by Jerrilyn Farmer • A Hollywood caterer to the stars who keeps finding her guests dead. Think twice before attending one of her parties!

➤ **DANNY BECKETT**, created by Tyler Dilts • A Long Beach police detective who's had more than his fair share of challenges and has the existential dread to prove it.

➤ **JUNIOR BENDER**, created by Timothy Hallinan • Junior is a crook's crook, a master burglar who moonlights as a private eye—for other criminals.

➤ **HARRY BOSCH**, created by Michael Connelly • Hieronymus "Harry" Bosch is an LAPD homicide detective with a troubled past, a loner's attitude, and a killer house in the Hollywood Hills.

➤ **ELVIS COLE**, created by Robert Crais • On the one hand, he's a Vietnam vet, a martial-arts pro, and a PI with an office near Musso's; on the other, he has a Mickey Mouse phone and quotes Jiminy Cricket.

➤ **CRUSH**, created by Phoef Sutton • This big, bald bodyguard/bouncer fled his Russian-mobster father to stay (more or less) on the right side of the law.

➤ **ALEX DELAWARE**, created by Jonathan Kellerman • A child psychologist turned forensic pathologist, Delaware is more of a sensitive, modern detective than a tough guy.

➤ **AARON GUNNER**, created by Gar Anthony Haywood • A regular-Joe guy in South L.A. who runs a private-detective business out of the back of a barbershop and does his best thinking at the Acey Deuce bar.

➤ **CHARLIE HOOD**, created by T. Jefferson Parker • An L.A. County sheriff's deputy who's attached to the ATF, investigating border crimes involving drugs, guns, and money.

➤ **BENJAMIN JUSTICE**, created by John Morgan Wilson • A disgraced crime reporter in West Hollywood, struggling to recover from the death of his lover from AIDS, attempts to right some wrongs he encounters while pulling his life together.

➤ **IRENE KELLY**, created by Jan Burke • An intrepid investigative reporter in a fictional town modeled after Long Beach. (Burke is a well-respected advocate for access to forensic science.)

➤ **MUNCH MANCINI**, created by Barbara Seranella • An ex-con and hardscrabble auto mechanic who has kicked a heroin addiction to make a new life for herself in Los Angeles.

➤ **PHILIP MARLOWE**, created by Raymond Chandler • The quintessential noir private eye.

➤ **LOU NORTON**, created by Rachel Howzell Hall • Elouise "Lou" Norton is a homicide detective in L.A.'s Southwest division who, like Harry Bosch, has both baggage and intense determination to find the truth.

➤ **ISAIAH QUINTABE (IQ)**, created by Joe Ide • An homage to Sherlock Holmes, if he were an orphaned African American teenager living in an east Long Beach hood.

➤ **EASY RAWLINS**, created by Walter Mosley • Watts resident Ezekiel "Easy" Rawlins is a World War II vet working as an unlicensed private eye in L.A. from the 1940s through the '60s.

➤ **DAVIE RICHARDS**, created by Patricia Smiley • She's a westsider, a millennial, and a second-generation homicide detective for the LAPD.

➤ **WOLLIE SHELLEY**, created by Harley Jane Kozak • How many amateur sleuths pay their rent by working as a greeting-card artist?

➤ **JUNIPER SONG**, created by Steph Cha • A smart, millennial, Korean American who's apprenticing as a private investigator and whose hero is Philip Marlowe.

➤ **NAN VINING**, created by Dianne Emley • This Pasadena homicide detective and single mom is haunted by an assault that almost took her life.

DETECTIVES ON L.A.

In L.A. people don't have time to stop: anywhere they have to go they go there in a car. The poorest man has a car in Los Angeles: he might not have a roof over his head but he has a car. And he knows where he's going too.

— EASY RAWLINS (Walter Mosley),
Devil in a Blue Dress (1990)

The thought of driving all that way to Glendale and then, in three hours, driving back over the hill into Los Angeles made Colin as weepy as a pastor's wife in a strip club.

— LOU NORTON (Rachel Howzell Hall),
Land of Shadows (2014)

I thought of the poor tourists with their rental cars sitting in traffic from Brentwood to downtown, from Hollywood to Disneyland, going home to cold climates and rejecting sunny California because of a fundamental misunderstanding of this city. Our United Neighborhoods of Los Angeles, each one its own universe if not its own island. I'd spent more time in Connecticut than I ever would in Venice, even if I died a white-haired woman fifteen miles away.

— JUNIPER SONG (Steph Cha),
Dead Soon Enough (2015)

Trying to get information out of a Los Angeles lawyer was like opening a can of sardines without a key.

— LEW ARCHER (Ross Macdonald),
The Archer Files (2015)

THE DAY OF THE DISSATISFIED WRITER NATHANAEL WEST

AT THE BEGINNING of Nathanael West's *The Day of the Locust*, often cited as the best Los Angeles novel by those who prefer a pessimistic view of the city, protagonist Tod Hackett takes the Red Car to Vine Street on his way home from the movie studio where he works as a background painter (the job pays the bills while he tries to paint his artistic masterpiece). Today the Red and Yellow cars are long gone, killed by the automobile industry, but fortunately the still-growing Metro system's Red Line has a stop right at Hollywood and Vine. So I rode the Red Line to that stop and set off in search of Hackett's Hollywood of the 1930s.

Walking north into the hills from the Metro station, I went first to Ivar, the street on which Hackett lives when he first moves to L.A. In some cases, as with Ivar, West used the actual name of a street or location; other times, he'd make up a name for a place that was inspired by something real. Perhaps he was delineating between places he described just as they were and places he changed for the sake of fiction—that is, if he was adding imaginary details. Maybe that's reading too much into it. What I do know is that he specifically referred to a hotel named the Chateau Mirabella on Ivar Avenue, so I climbed up Ivar from Hollywood, looking for a building like the Mirabella—not to mention West's own apartment.

Ivar, like many streets in this neighborhood, was changed after West's day with the construction of the 101. It's an uphill walk to the northern end of the street, just below Franklin. At the top of the street are clear views into the Hollywood Hills, of the 101, and of Franklin

Then again, you never knew in Los Angeles what you might find around the next corner. You could be in the quiet, sunny, and gritty desolation of a block like this one moment, and find yourself on a tree-lined, shady, and glimmering block of apartments the next.

— HÉCTOR TOBAR, *The Barbarian Nurseries* (2011)

Avenue ferrying people east and west under the freeway. This short bit of street, between Yucca and the curve at its end, feels like a captured moment from Hollywood's past, with old trees and 1920s/'30s-era Spanish and faux Tudor apartment buildings, including one that could easily pass for the Chateau Mirabella, mixed in with a couple of boxy '60s structures. When he first moved to L.A., West himself lived on this very block, in a studio apartment at 1817 N. Ivar. (He later moved a little farther up into the hills, to a 1924 house at 6614 Cahuenga Terrace that still stands today.) Despite the modern cars, I could picture Hackett, Homer Simpson, and West himself bustling to and from their homes. (Regarding Simpson: Yes, that's the name of another key character, and it's not a total coincidence that Matt Groening used the name, although his father was also named Homer.)

I walked back down Ivar to Sunset Boulevard and headed westward, like Hackett and his Hollywood-fringe compatriots did when they were going to Mrs. Jenning's brothel. I turned right at La Brea, a street to which Hackett's love interest, Faye, drives Hackett and his rival for her affections, Earle, to dinner—but rather than go to dinner, they keep going into the hills to Earle's makeshift encampment in one of the canyons, on fictional Zacarias Street. The canyon where Earle and Miguel have their camp is now full of upscale houses, as are all the canyons in the Hollywood Hills. Today's homeless encampments are under and alongside freeways and vacant lots in the flats, not up in the hills.

Since it would be impossible to find the kind of homeless camp that Earle and Miguel had, I turned east on Hollywood Boulevard to visit the Chinese Theatre. Kahn's Persian Palace in *The Day of the Locust* was clearly the Chinese Theatre—once Grauman's, then Mann's, and now the rather less romantic TCL Chinese Theatre.

During a film premiere at the Persian Palace, the novel reaches its cataclysmic zenith, and as I wandered around the theater's handprint-decorated forecourt on a weekday morning, that scene came vividly to life in my mind's eye. It would be even easier to imagine on the right night, when you might walk past crowds of people waiting outside for hours for a premiere and a chance to see movie stars. In this key scene, the crowd is restive and catches Hackett in a melee. West writes, "The crowd in front of the theatre had charged. He was surrounded by churning legs and feet. He pulled himself erect by grabbing a man's coat, then let himself be carried along backwards in a long, curving swoop." It's not hard to sink into West's cynical view

of Hollywood—he used the lives of his prosaic Hollywood workers as a metaphor for the death of dreams and a satiric commentary on the shallowness and vanity of pop culture—when encountering the tawdriness of Hollywood Boulevard, with its junky souvenir shops, tourist-clogged sidewalks, and wax museum–style amusements. Or maybe it still feels full of life and possibility for those who visit for the first time. In any case, it was a relief to leave without being trampled, or without retreating so far into my own head as to be cut loose from reality—the way Hackett becomes after the premiere riot, when he's in a police car and starts shrieking siren noises.

As a postscript, *The Day of the Locust* may be a literary staple today, often taught in literature courses, but it was a failure when published, selling fewer than 1,500 copies in its first year. With a dark irony that would have suited the novel, West never saw the success that was headed his way—he and his wife were killed in a car accident a year after the book came out, apparently because he was driving distractedly after just having heard that his good friend F. Scott Fitzgerald had died of a heart attack the day before.

WRITERS WHO HATE L.A.

The world's biggest third-class city.

— JOHN D. MACDONALD, *A Deadly Shade of Gold* (1965)

Everything in Los Angeles is too large, too loud and usually banal in concept... The plastic asshole of the world.

— WILLIAM FAULKNER, source unknown

They are a very decent, generous lot of people out here and they don't expect you to listen. Always remember that, dear boy. It's the secret of social ease in this country. They talk entirely for their own pleasure. Nothing they say is designed to be heard.

— EVELYN WAUGH, *The Loved One* (1948)

It is redundant to die in Los Angeles.

— TRUMAN CAPOTE, source unknown

Los Angeles is the least accessible and therefore the worst reported of American cities. It is not available to the walker in the city. There is no place where the natives gather. Distance obliterates unity and community. This inaccessibility means that the contemporary De Tocqueville on a layover between planes can define Los Angeles only in terms of his own culture shock.

— JOHN GREGORY DUNNE, "Eureka! A Celebration of California," an essay in *Unknown California* (1985)

There was nothing wrong with Southern California that a rise in the ocean level wouldn't cure.

— ROSS MACDONALD, *The Drowning Pool* (1950)

Where everybody wears rhinestones in their glasses to show that they own an airplane factory.

—S.J. PERELMAN,
The Rising Gorge (1961)

Los Angeles was the kind of place where everybody was from somewhere else and nobody really dropped anchor. It was a transient place. People drawn by the dream, people running from the nightmare. Twelve million people and all of them ready to make a break for it if necessary. Figuratively, literally, metaphorically—any way you want to look at it— everybody in L.A. keeps a bag packed. Just in case.

— MICHAEL CONNELLY, *The Brass Verdict* (2008)

I'm shocked by anyone who doesn't consider Los Angeles to be anything less than a bozo-saturated hellhole.

— CHUCK KLOSTERMAN, *Killing Yourself to Live* (2005)

WRITERS WHO LOVE L.A.

The stars stepped out of their limos onto the klieg-lighted sidewalk of Hollywood Boulevard for the movie-palace premiere, braving the surge of besieging fans penned in by police sawhorses; I saw newsreels of these apparitions. The gods of high culture had disembarked from Europe to dwell, almost incognito, among the lemon trees and beach boys and neo-Bauhaus architecture and fantasy hamburgers; they weren't, I was sure, supposed to have something like fans, who would seek to intrude on their privacy.

— Susan Sontag,
Debriefing: Collected Stories (1961)

Virginia Woolf tantalizes me. I wish I could write like that. She is in love with London and I am in love with L.A., but London has seasons and this giant history and stratas of society... She wouldn't like L.A. but maybe she'd forgive me for loving it anyway.

— Eve Babitz, *Eve's Hollywood* (1974)

Finding your L.A. means giving yourself over to the city—its contours and riddles. When you do, you'll feel it; there's an aspect of L.A. that slips in under your skin. Less attitude than predilection, or frame of mind. It seeps in. Like the soot that drifts in, that finds its way through tiny gaps in your windows, the grit that powders your floors after even the mildest Santa Anas. You don't see it drifting in, accumulating, but you note the traces later. Sometimes it just startles you.

— Lynell George, *After/Image* (2018)

Jacaranda trees thrive in Los Angeles, like blondes and Mexicans. There's no getting away from them, not even in my dreams.

— BRANDO SKYHORSE, *Madonnas of Echo Park* (2010)

In the movie version, Skid Row was played by 1960s Bunker Hill and age twelve was played by a grasshopper flying in a summer field. Sweetness careened down the streets in buses and trolleys.

— SESSHU FOSTER, *City of the Future* (2018)

Upon their arrival in the city, Fong See and Ticie first went to Chinatown, where they saw sights reminiscent of Sacramento's Chinese quarter. Street vendors offered sugared coconut shavings, rice cakes, and roasted melon seeds. Signboards beckoned customers with tantalizing promises. Men might find a cure at an apothecary with a sign that read "Benevolence and Longevity Hall"... The air itself seemed to beckon with the aromatic odors of roast pork, duck eggs preserved in oil, dried abalone, and cuttlefish.

— LISA SEE, *On Gold Mountain* (1995)

Long before he set foot in this country, Antonio felt that he knew California because he'd seen it come to life over and over again on his television set. In Antonio's homeland, the words "Los Angeles" sparkled, like sunlight glimmering off a mountain lake.

— HÉCTOR TOBAR, *The Tattooed Soldier* (1998)

ESSENTIAL BOOKSTORES

The usual caveat: We hope and pray these are in business when you read this, but we can't make any promises.

➤ **ANGEL CITY BOOKS & RECORDS**, 218 Pier St., Santa Monica • The last indie bookstore in Santa Monica carries, buys, and trades used books and records, including some cool vintage finds.

➤ **ARCANA BOOKS ON THE ARTS**, 8675 Washington Blvd., Culver City • This impressive visual arts bookstore in the historic Helms Bakery complex contains both new and used books.

➤ **ARTBOOK @ HAUSER & WIRTH L.A.**, 917 E. 3rd St., Downtown • Housed in the L.A. branch of Hauser & Wirth's global galleries, Artbook specializes in female-focused titles and a rotating selection of books on contemporary art and culture.

➤ **BOOK SHOW**, 5503 N. Figueroa St., Highland Park • Besides a solid selection of quirky and well-curated used books and gifts, Book Show offers regular readings and performances in Highland Park.

➤ **BOOK SOUP**, 8818 Sunset Blvd., West Hollywood • A Hollywood staple specializing in film, art, entertainment, and literary titles, it also hosts an A-list roster of author events and clientele.

➤ **CHEVALIER'S**, 126 N. Larchmont Blvd., Hancock Park • L.A.'s oldest bookstore has a carefully curated roster of new books in two rooms and a vibrant schedule of events—the small-town-feel shop attracts big-name authors.

➤ **CHILDREN'S BOOK WORLD**, 10580 Pico Blvd., West L.A. • Opened in 1986, this westside institution boasts regular weekend storytime and more than 80,000 titles for children (as well as parents and teachers).

➤ **DARK DELICACIES**, 822 N. Hollywood Way, Burbank • Located in Burbank's Magnolia Park (and rescued from closure in 2019 with help from Guillermo del Toro and Neil Gaiman), this delight of an indie specializes in all things horror.

At Chevalier's, L.A. authors Abbi Waxman and Hilary Liftin pack the house for a reading and conversation.

➤ **DIESEL, A BOOKSTORE,** Brentwood Country Mart, 225 26th St., Santa Monica • With a remarkably diverse range of titles and events for such a small store, Diesel is the westside book lover's go-to hangout.

➤ **ESO WON BOOKS,** 4327 Degnan Blvd., Leimart Park • One of the oldest black-owned bookstores in the country, Eso Won showcases titles about (and written by) African American authors and is known for its many events.

➤ **FLINTRIDGE BOOKSTORE & COFFEEHOUSE,** 1010 Foothill Blvd., La Cañada • On-site self-publishing (via an Espresso machine), a busy events schedule, and a cozy café are the highlights of this well-stocked community bookstore.

➤ **GATSBY BOOKS,** 5535 E. Spring St., Long Beach • This Long Beach literary gem boasts new and gently used books, a congenial staff, and a furry, four-legged shop associate.

Hennessy + Ingalls

➤ **THE GETTY STORE,** The Getty Center, 1200 Getty Center Dr., Brentwood • Full of books, jewelry, gifts, and apparel that echo the rich art and culture found in the museum's galleries.

➤ **HAMMER STORE,** UCLA Hammer Museum, 10899 Wilshire Blvd., Westwood • The Hammer offers free admission and this carefully curated store, which counts plenty of books among its mix of goods.

➤ **HENNESSY + INGALLS,** 300 S. Santa Fe Ave., Downtown • A bright, modern Arts District space for books and magazines on art, architecture, design, and culture.

➤ **THE HUNTINGTON STORE,** 1151 Oxford Rd., San Marino • One of the largest museum gift shops in the region, it carries a beautiful array of books on the arts, design, gardens, travel, and more, including for children.

➤ **THE ILIAD BOOKSHOP,** 5400 Cahuenga Blvd., North Hollywood • More than 150,000 used books, with a focus on literature and the arts, are shelved in inviting warrens with comfy couches so you can sit and read for a spell.

➤ **JAPANESE AMERICAN NATIONAL MUSEUM STORE**, 100 N. Central Ave., Little Tokyo •
After a worthwhile visit to the museum, you'll find a broad selection of books, as well as ceramics, gifts, and
home goods.

➤ **KINOKUNIYA**, 123 Astronaut E.S. Onizuka St., Little Tokyo; 3760 S. Centinela Ave., Mar Vista •
The L.A. branch of the Japanese chain, with Asian-centric books, manga, magazines, and stationery.

➤ **LACMA STORE**, LACMA, 5905 Wilshire Blvd., Miracle Mile • From art books and exhibition catalogs to
guidebooks and children's titles, the LACMA Store has an extensive book selection.

➤ **LARRY EDMUNDS**, 6644 Hollywood Blvd., Hollywood • A must-see for showbiz junkies, this Hollywood
institution has hundreds of thousands of movie and theater books, scripts, plays, posters, photographs,
and more.

➤ **THE LAST BOOKSTORE**, 453 S. Spring
St., Downtown • The oft-Instagrammed book
tunnel lives upstairs (as does the Spring Arts
Collective), but you'll want to explore every
nook and cranny of this vast space in a historic
former bank building that now features new
and used books, vinyl, and other media.

➤ **LIBRERIA L.A.**, Second Home, 1370 N.
St. Andrews Pl., East Hollywood • The L.A.
offshoot of the London store of the same
name, providing a highly curated selection
of new books grouped by theme, rather than
genre, in a small space on Second Home's
Hollywood campus.

➤ **LIBROS SCHMIBROS**, 103 N. Boyle Ave., Boyle Heights • It's mostly a lending library (see page 101),
but this wonderful nonprofit also sells used books at very low prices, with a mission of getting books into the
hands of its neighbors.

➤ **MYSTERY PIER BOOKS**, 8826 Sunset Blvd., West Hollywood • With first editions, rare books, and signed
volumes, as well as a particular focus on mystery, literature, and books that have become movies, this shop is
heaven for the collector.

➤ NORTON SIMON MUSEUM STORE, 411 W. Colorado Blvd., Pasadena • A thoughtful selection of art books, books tied to special exhibitions, prints, posters, and gifts, plus a commendable children's section.

➤ ONCE UPON A TIME, 2207 Honolulu Ave., Montrose • It claims to be the country's oldest children's bookstore, which is hard to fact-check, but we love the small-town Montrose setting, the warm vibe, and the small, superbly curated selection of books for adults, so we'll take the claim on faith.

➤ OTHER BOOKS, 2006 E. Cesar E. Chavez Ave., Boyle Heights • A collaboration by Seite Books and Kaya Press, this space hosts events and carries new and used books, comics, and zines, emphasizing writers and artists of color, literature in translation, alternative comics, POC history, and small-press titles.

➤ PAGE AGAINST THE MACHINE, 2714 E. 4th St., Long Beach • In a mere 400 square feet, this newcomer to the indie bookstore scene has a social-justice ethos and a super-smart reader for a proprietor.

➤ PAGES, 904 Manhattan Ave., Manhattan Beach • Run by longtime locals, this friendly general bookstore keeps adults and kids in the South Bay reading, with engaging events and weekly storytime for kids.

➤ POP-HOP BOOKSTORE, 5002 York Blvd., Highland Park • Celebrating small presses and local zines and goods, Pop-Hop carries new and used books, as well as many art publications.

➤ THE RIPPED BODICE, 3806 Main St., Culver City • All romance, all the time, founded and run by two women whose love for romance fiction is so deep and well-informed that they now have a development deal at Sony Studios.

➤ SECRET HEADQUARTERS, 3817 W. Sunset Blvd., Silver Lake • A comic book lover's dream, filled with classics, indies, contemporaries, and zines, as well as a highly knowledgeable staff.

Skylight's natural light and indoor tree encourage readers to settle in for a spell.

➤ THE SHOP AT THE BROAD, Broad Museum, 221 S. Grand Ave., Downtown • Accessible without a museum ticket, the Shop at the Broad has a wide range of art and culture books among the gifts, prints, and limited-edition sculptures for sale.

➤ SKYLIGHT BOOKS, 1818 N. Vermont Ave., Los Feliz • One of L.A.'s smartest, most literary bookstores, with strong selections of poetry, indie-press books, works by L.A. authors, and an annex showcasing fantastic visual books. The events roster is first-rate.

Community-focused book events are essential to Tía Chucha's mission.

➤ **SMALL WORLD BOOKS, 1407 Ocean Front Walk, Venice** • A family-owned Venice staple since 1976—grab a coffee at the attached Sidewalk Café, browse the impressive selection, and say hello to the kitty assistant.

➤ **STORIES, 1716 Sunset Blvd., Echo Park** • In the heart of Echo Park (and right next door to 826LA and its Time Travel Mart), Stories buys and sells new and used books and has a nifty little café in the back.

➤ **TÍA CHUCHA'S, 13197 Gladstone Ave., Sylmar** • With a diverse offering of books, as well as programming in music, art, and writing, this community center was founded by poet and author Luis J. Rodriguez.

➤ **VROMAN'S BOOKSTORE, 695 E. Colorado Blvd., Pasadena** • A beloved institution with a vast title selection, knowledgeable staff, and celebrated children's section, this is the oldest and largest bookstore in Southern California; it also has an outpost of Jones Coffee and a new wine bar. A smaller branch is located in Hastings Ranch/east Pasadena, at 3729 E. Foothill Blvd.

➤ **WHITMORE RARE BOOKS, 121 Union St., Pasadena** • This jewel of a shop in Old Pasadena is almost like an art gallery, with gorgeous editions of classic titles on display.

Vroman's has two stories of shelves packed with a superb collection of new titles.

The bookstore was a treasure chest, stuffed with books by publishers and writers who long ago had failed. This was the last place to find them, a cemetery of sorts. It was her favorite place in all Los Angeles.

— MICHELLE TEA, *Black Wave* (2016)

READ ME, LOS ANGELES

WITCH OF ECHO PARK
AMBER BENSON

IT WAS A SUNNY SPRING AFTERNOON at Valerie Confections in Echo Park, which is just a few blocks from the homes of the titular witches from Amber Benson's *Witches of Echo Park*, the first in the Echo Park Coven trilogy of books about a coven of witches whose magic affects the world. This bakery/café was a perfect choice for an interview with the actress and author because she lived across the street when she wrote the novels.

Cold drinks in hand, we settled outside to watch the neighborhood pass by while we discussed setting a fantasy series in L.A. and, specifically, in this area. "I fell in love with Echo Park when I moved here," Benson said. After living in Angelino Heights for a few years, she relocated to Westlake, near MacArthur Park, but was soon drawn back to Echo Park. "I actually lived in that building for three years," she said, gesturing to an apartment complex across the street from our table.

"There's something really magical about Echo Park," she explained. "You walk around Sunset and see botanicas sandwiched in between little hipster coffee shops and vintage stores, and there's Stories, the bookstore. There are the hills, which were very bohemian in the '40s and '50s. There are stair streets and these amazing little bungalows with fairy lights. It's just an incredible place."

Though Echo Park is known today for gentrification and hipness, Benson has long been intrigued by its bohemian past; the Semi-Tropic Spiritualist camp used to host bonfires and naked dancing up in the hills, and Red Hill attracted artists and creative people during the height of McCarthyism. This mystical past made it easy for her to imagine witches and magic existing alongside the coffeehouses and vegan bistros that populate the area today.

Benson credits another writer for her fascination with L.A. "I loved *Weetzie Bat*," she said. "I fell in love with L.A. reading those books. There's something super magical about the world and the characters that Francesca Lia Block crafted, and the book has such a feeling of place. There's such a magical realism to Los Angeles, and I wanted

Photo by Lindsay Byrnes

An Elysian Park grove that just might host a coven.

to capture that." Echo Park turned out to be the ideal setting for Benson's particular interests. "There were three things I wanted to write about," she said. "First, women's relationships with each other because when I moved to Echo Park, I ended up with this amazing crew of creative ladies. Second, I wanted to write about it because I was just obsessed: When I moved here—I knew that this was my place. The third thing I wanted to write about was witches."

Benson's fantasy trilogy is rich with references to real, specific locations and landmarks, like a grove in Elysian Park where her coven meets. She talked about a few more places that appear in the novels: "There's an old Jewish cemetery with eucalyptus, and there's all kinds of crazy stuff in Elysian Park that I crafted into my world. In the books there's a rock that is shaped like a dragon-snake, which is a real thing. And the house on Curran is a house that I tried to buy once." Another location is a coffeehouse that she said is a combination of Fix and Chango. "I took both of them as inspiration," she said, "which was cool because I wrote the books in both of those places."

Fix and Chango are closed now, only two of the many businesses that have vanished in recent years. "It was not as hip when I first moved here," Benson said. "It's changed a lot, for better or worse. With gentrification comes the loss of a way of life and a culture. What I think is nice about the eastside of L.A. is that it's at least trying to hang on to that culture."

One of the café employees stopped to chat about Benson's role on *Buffy the Vampire Slayer*, and I asked Benson about the transition from acting to writing novels. "I've always written poems, plays, and stories," she said. "I started writing with Chris Golden, and we created an animated series for the BBC, *Ghosts of Albion*. I'd met him because of *Buffy*. I remember when we were talking to Random House about novelizing the series and our editor, Steve, said, 'I just have to ask—you're actually writing these, right? Chris isn't doing all this?'"

A friend gave Benson photos of Chango as it looked when she wrote her trilogy there. Thoughtfulness like this is part of the supportive writing culture she's found in L.A., one that goes far beyond TV and film. "I'm part of a writers' group," she said. "People write books set

She could taste the past in her mouth, smell it in the air around her as she wandered the streets and stairways of Laveta Terrace, Baxter, Clinton, and Curran, each stairwell a link to the landlocked hill homes that were built, so oddly, without street access. Sweat-soaked limbs and squeaking sneakers were her only companions as she trudged up and down the roughly curving hill streets.

— AMBER BENSON, *The Witches of Echo Park* (2015)

here, they're writing plays set here. Comic books. Graphic novels. Creative people are creative across the board now." She said when she first started writing fiction, some people who thought of her as an actor were uncertain. "I like to say that I took all the dues I paid trying to be an actor for twentysomething years and cheated the publishing system by crediting those dues in this other industry. *Buffy* was the reason doors opened for me that would never have opened as easily. It allowed me to grow and become the writer that I am." She's written more books, most recently one for children.

Taking advantage of the beautiful weather, we decamped from our sidewalk table and walked up Echo Park Avenue to the house that she once wanted to buy—the one that became the center of *Witches of Echo Park*. It's a lovely uphill walk to a home closed off from the street by a wall and solid doors. "I want to root my work in a reality," Benson said as we peeked through the gap between the doors. It was an obstructed view, which only added to the sense of magic she gave it in her writing, and for a moment I felt invited to step into the world she had created.

WRITING WORKSHOPS

If all this reading about L.A.'s book culture makes you want to try your hand at writing, Southern California has plenty of workshops and programs to help you hone your craft. Here are a few of our favorites around town and online. If you're more ambitious, check out the MFA programs at CalArts, Otis, Antioch, UC Irvine, UC Riverside, and Cal State Long Beach, and the PhD program at USC.

- **inspiration2publication**
  - inspiration2publication.wordpress.com
  - Affordable book coaching and creative writing classes in all genres, offered 100 percent online

- **UCLA Extension Writers' Program**
  - writers.uclaextension.edu
  - Peerless continuing education program for creative writing and screenwriting, offering a certificate track, à la carte classes, retreats, master classes, and more, both at UCLA and online

- **Writers at Work**
  - writersatwork.com
  - Terry Wolverton's long-running creative writing workshop in Silver Lake for writers of poetry, short fiction, and book-length work

- **Writing Workshops Los Angeles**
  - writingworkshopsla.com
  - For poets and prose writers, WWLA hosts classes in various locations, as well as one-on-one education, manuscript consultations, and book coaching

WEETZIE BAT & HER DANGEROUS ANGELS FRANCESCA LIA BLOCK

FRANCESCA LIA BLOCK was kind enough to invite me to her home. It was fitting, since home, as represented by Weetzie Bat's cottage, is one of the enduring images in Block's most famous series of novels. But while Weetzie's little house is on Sweetzer Avenue in West Hollywood, Block's sits on a quiet street in Culver City. And while Block is often conflated with her beloved character, once we settled down to talk about her life in L.A. and her writing, it was clear that they're quite distinct. Weetzie is a product of Block's fertile imagination—an imagination that has resulted in some thirty books.

Block's lifetime in Los Angeles has strongly impacted her writing. She was raised in Studio City, the daughter of a painter/screenwriter father and a mother who loved poetry and dancing. "My parents had lived on the L.A. side of Laurel Canyon, and they moved to the Valley side when I was small," she said. "I started going over Laurel Canyon back to the L.A. side as a teenager because it was a lot more interesting—more so because I lived a little bit away from it."

Block explained that her parents' creativity and bohemian attitudes inspired her development as a writer, and she's grateful that they encouraged her. Like so many savvy young writers, she started out writing what she knew: Los Angeles. "I found a lot of inspiration in L.A.," she said. "It became a muse." Her way of writing about her city—"where it was hot and cool, glam and slam, rich and trashy, devils and angels" (*Weetzie Bat*)—is so evocative that it has propelled many young women to move here since *Weetzie Bat* was published in 1989.

While many of Block's novels are grounded in the "real" L.A., a current of fabulism also runs through her work. This magic stems from her personal worldview: "It's just the way I see the world. I think it's a survival mechanism—seeing the world around you with a creative spin on things makes life more livable, especially as it gets more complicated." L.A. itself influenced the wondrous bent to her work. "I think the city reflects that sort of magic and inspires that sort of thinking," she said. "It's the film industry and the dream of it and the landscape—the way the city and nature are interwoven." They combine to feed the sense of unexpected possibilities in Block's fiction.

Almost every setting in *Weetzie Bat* is based on a real place, "even down to Vixanne's Jayne Mansfield fan club witches' coven," Block said. "I don't remember where it was exactly, but when I was a teenager, I saw a flyer for a Jayne Mansfield fan club and we went to it. It was this strange little bungalow in Hollywood where they played Jayne Mansfield movies, and it was full of weird, drug addict–looking people."

She based Grandma Fifi's cottage on the fairy-tale-style cottages found in such older neighborhoods as Los Feliz, Hollywood, and West Hollywood. "I knew in my mind the type of building Weetzie lived in, inspired by the midcentury-modern dingbat apartments around Fairfax," Block said. "Everything I described is based on a specific place, like Hollywood in Miniature or the carousel on Santa Monica Pier." Making Fifi's home on Sweetzer a storybook cottage adds whimsical fantasy to the story, a fantasy that expands when teenage Weetzie inherits it and moves in after Fifi dies.

If Los Angeles is a woman reclining billboard model with collagen-puffed lips and silicone-inflated breasts, a woman in a magenta convertible with heart-shaped sunglasses and cotton candy hair; if Los Angeles is this woman, then the San Fernando Valley is her teenybopper sister.

— Francesca Lia Block, *I Was a Teenage Fairy* (1998)

As in so many of the novels preceding Block's work in the Los Angeles canon, there are characters who have been burned out by the Hollywood system. In *Weetzie Bat*, it's the character known only as My Secret Agent Lover Man. But the overall tone of her modern-classic novel remains hopeful, embracing beauty over bitterness. That juxtaposition finds its inspiration in the city itself: "Even in the landscape, the jacaranda trees and the freeways coexist. We have a beautiful sky because of the air pollution."

Block said she's an introvert, but she's found her L.A. writing community naturally over the years. "We've met through events, friends of friends, and teaching at Writing Workshops L.A.," she explained. "I've been on panels with other writers at festivals. It's not a huge community in L.A., so you end up with everyone being in touch in some way."

Block wrote *Weetzie Bat* for adults, but it ended up finding a home with teens and young adults. Many of her other novels, including the *Weetzie Bat* sequels, the short-story collection *Girl Goddess #9*, and the novel *Island of Excess Love*, were all marketed as young adult novels. Her most recent books, including *The Elementals*, have marked a return to fiction aimed at an adult audience. Block's work often exists in a liminal space, however, and she's let her publishers identify the audience. "I've written whatever I've wanted, and they've made decisions about it," she said. She also credited her first editor, Charlotte Zolotow (then at Harper & Row), for being "a radical children's publisher who was breaking barriers down." Zolotow allowed gay characters and complex family arrangements to be in a book aimed at teen readers. "I was lucky to have had an editor who got that to a younger audience.

"My audience now is mostly late thirties and forties—they've grown up with my work," she continued. "The loyal fans are now reading my book about raising my daughter when they're pregnant, and they're showing their children my books. I've never written for an age group, but for a certain type of person. I think my reader is an outsider—an artsy, humanistic kind of person. They can be thirteen or sixty."

As for her city, Block said, "I do think there's a lot of invention here, partly because of the movie industry and the 'Go West' sense of reinvention," noting that this spirit of invention is liberating for an author. "As an L.A. writer in my twenties, I didn't have to be a literary darling. I could just do my own weird little stuff. Now, of course, L.A.'s more literary—or rather, more people have realized that it always was—and so now there's more emphasis on its literary culture." Of course, that realization is due in part to L.A. writers like Block.

CHILDREN'S AUTHORS

Something about L.A. fuels the creativity of so many children's authors and illustrators. Here are just a few of the best known.

AUTHOR	➤	KNOWN FOR
JOHN ARCHAMBAULT	➤	Chicka Chicka Boom Boom
ELANA K. ARNOLD	➤	A Boy Called Bat / Question of Miracles
BETHANY BARTON	➤	This Monster Needs a Haircut / Give Bees a Chance
FRANK BEDDOR	➤	The Looking Glass Wars Trilogy / Hatter M Graphic Novel series
SAMANTHA BERGER	➤	Crankenstein
PSEUDONYMOUS BOSCH	➤	The Name of This Book Is Secret
EVE BUNTING	➤	Smoky Night / A Day's Work
STACIA DEUTSCH	➤	Girls Who Code series / Blast to the Past series
AMY EPHRON	➤	The Castle in the Mist series
MARLA FRAZEE	➤	All the World / Boss Baby / It Takes a Village
CARTER HIGGINS	➤	Bikes for Sale
JON KLASSEN	➤	I Want My Hat Back / We Found a Hat
D.J. MACHALE	➤	Pendragon series / SYLO Chronicles / Morpheus Road books
KERRY MADDEN-LUNSFORD	➤	Gentle's Holler
TAHEREH MAFI	➤	Furthermore / Whichwood
GEORGE McCLEMENTS	➤	Baron von Baddie and the Ice Ray Incident / Night of the Veggie Monster
MAILE MELOY	➤	Apothecary Trilogy
SHANNON MESSENGER	➤	Keepers of the Lost Cities
DANA MIDDLETON	➤	Open If You Dare
SUSAN PATRON	➤	Higher Power of Lucky
LEUYEN PHAM	➤	Princess in Black
DEAN PITCHFORD	➤	Nickle Bay Nick / Captain Nobody / The Big One-Oh
DAN SANTAT	➤	The Adventures of Beekle / After the Fall
DAVID SHANNON	➤	The No, David! books
HOLLY GOLDBERG SLOAN	➤	I'll Be There / Short / Counting by 7s
JANET TASHJIAN	➤	My Life series
EUGENE YELCHIN	➤	Breaking Stalin's Nose

THE LAND OF ETERNAL YOUTH: YOUNG ADULT LITERATURE IN L.A.

WHEN DOES THE MYTH of L.A. begin in readers' minds? For many, their image of the city is shaped by the books they read as teenagers. In addition to the kid-oriented TV shows that portray a mild, laugh-tracked version of L.A., it is books about the city that begin to form their perception of it.

Starting with Frederick Kohner's *Gidget*, L.A.'s youth culture was often depicted in idealized form for young readers dreaming of endless sunny days of surf and fun. (*Ramona*, starring a young woman, romanticized Southern California in the late 1800s.) *Gidget* picked up even more influence when it was turned into movies and a TV series, but its original form was a novel that sparked interest in kids from Nebraska to Nevada. The Donna Parker series of proto–young adult novels saw Donna take a trip to glamorous Hollywood, a trope that existed in many YA novels of the time. That Hollywood may have been full of excitement and fame, but it also often led to a message that the values of a small-town visitor were superior to those of louche Angelenos.

In the 1980s, Francine Pascal wrote the Sweet Valley High books, creating a fictional Southern California town that was a fantasy version of life near, but not *too* near, Los Angeles. Sweet Valley was an idyllic town, except when an important lesson was to be imparted via a teen's cocaine death or plane crash. It, too, established the idea of Southern California as a place that offered a beautiful life, if only one could find Sweet Valley. The Baby-Sitters Club series, one of SVH's contemporaries, even included books that took place in L.A., when BSC member Dawn returned to the West Coast to visit her father, occasionally bringing the rest of her friends along.

Those views of Southern California were safely sanitized for young readers who knew little of the real place. They served as continuations of the propaganda pushed out by business leaders and real estate developers in the early twentieth century, promising a golden land of sunshine, oranges, and ceaseless opportunities. While those opportunities materialized for some, for others they did not. This led to a counterbalance of writers who sought to show the unglamorous underbelly of the city, from John Fante and Charles Bukowski to Raymond

Chandler and Janet Fitch.

L.A.'s young adult literature didn't veer as far into the dark as books by those writers did, but a more realistic view slowly emerged as the field matured. The seminal text of that transitionary era was a novel that was not intended for young readers. Francesca Lia Block wrote *Weetzie Bat* for adults, but when editor Charlotte Zolotow acquired it, she realized that teenagers would connect best with the magical vision of L.A. that Block conveyed.

Weetzie Bat zooms through the same brightly colored L.A. that YA books had previously portrayed, but she also encounters death, heartbreak, betrayal, queer friends facing discrimi-

They didn't even realize where they were living. They didn't care that Marilyn's prints were practically in their backyard at Grauman's; that you could buy tomahawks and plastic palm tree wallets at Farmers Market, and the wildest, cheapest cheese and bean and hot dog and pastrami burritos at Oki Dogs; that the waitresses wore skates at the Jetsons-style Tiny Naylor's; that there was a fountain that turned tropical soda-pop colors, and a canyon where Jim Morrison and Houdini used to live, and all-night potato knishes at Canter's, and not too far away was Venice, with columns, and canals, even, like the real Venice but maybe cooler because of the surfers.

— Francesca Lia Block, *Weetzie Bat* (1989)

nation, and the disappointment of failed Hollywood careers. Even with its magical realism, the story created an image of the city that felt deeply true, and many young women say they moved to L.A. because of that novel.

As young adult literature continues to evolve, so do the YA authors in Los Angeles. Many of the most prolific members of that community write about fantastical worlds that are not veiled visions of Los Angeles, but nevertheless, they are Angelenos, and they come together to support one another and the literary life of the city. One of the great contributions to that literary scene has been the establishment of YALLWEST, an annual YA literature festival. It's the West Coast offshoot of the original YALLFEST. YALLWEST was founded in Santa Monica by Margaret Stohl and Melissa de la Cruz, who wanted to bring the festival close to their homes. In addition to attracting YA and middle-grade authors from around the country, it has played host to such Angelenos as Gretchen McNeil, Ransom Riggs, Tahereh Mafi, Maurene Goo, Nicola Yoon, David Yoon, and Leigh Bardugo. These writers also encourage and support one another at book events throughout the year. At one recent gathering, Robin Benway, the author of *Emmy & Oliver* and *Far from the Tree*, thanked "an incredibly generous, talented, and funny-as-hell group of YA writers here in Los Angeles."

Their love for the city doesn't always mean L.A. locations appear in their books, but when they do, it's a Los Angeles less idealized and more faithful to the verisimilitude that today's YA readers demand. Goo, for example, writes in *The Way You Make Me Feel*, "Despite what it means to popular culture, Sunset Boulevard isn't a glamorous street littered with movie stars driving around in convertibles or something. For one thing, Sunset runs here all the way from the beach. It's like twenty-two miles long." She draws a realistic picture of a city populated by kids of all ethnicities, and she avoids the cliché of focusing on the Hollywood machine.

That isn't to say that some L.A. authors aren't still examining the toll that celebrity and the quest for fame take on young people. In Zara Lisbon's *Fake Plastic Girl*, the protagonist begins on the outskirts of celebrity before becoming fast friends with a child star and observes, "Growing up in Los Angeles with two parents who rubbed elbows with celebrities—Mom adored it, Dad resented it—put me in an odd *Twilight Zone*–style limbo between two different worlds: the world of fame and the world of anonymity." That's a place that many Angelenos have found themselves in, and a place that many visitors want to explore.

YA AUTHORS

As we've said earlier, we can't possibly include all the literary talents in this huge city, but these folks are particularly notable swimmers in the young adult fiction pool.

AUTHOR	➤	KNOWN FOR
ELANA K. ARNOLD	➤	What Girls Are Made Of / Damsel
VICTORIA AVEYARD	➤	Red Queen series
LEIGH BARDUGO	➤	Shadow & Bone / Six of Crows / Ninth House
ROBIN BENWAY	➤	Emmy & Oliver / Far from the Tree
JULIE BERRY	➤	All The Truth That's in Me / Lovely War / The Passion of Dolssa
CECIL CASTELLUCCI	➤	Beige
STEPHEN CHBOSKY	➤	The Perks of Being a Wallflower
BRANDY COLBERT	➤	Little & Lion
MELISSA DE LA CRUZ	➤	Something in Between
MAURENE GOO	➤	The Way You Make Me Feel
EMILY ZIFF GRIFFIN	➤	Light Years
ZARA LISBON	➤	Fake Plastic Girl
MARIE LU	➤	Legend
TAHEREH MAFI	➤	Shatter Me series / A Very Large Expanse of Sea
MORGAN MATSON	➤	Save the Date
GRETCHEN McNEIL	➤	#murdertrending / Get Even / Ten
PATRICK NESS	➤	Chaos Walking series / A Monster Calls / More Than This
RANSOM RIGGS	➤	Peculiar Children series
LILLIAM RIVERA	➤	Dealing in Dreams
ROMINA RUSSELL	➤	Zodiac series
ADAM SILVERA	➤	They Both Die at the End / History Is All You Left Me
ANDREW SMITH	➤	Grasshopper Jungle / Winger
MARGARET STOHL	➤	Beautiful Creature series
JEN WANG	➤	The Prince and the Dressmaker / Stargazing
DAVID YOON	➤	Frankly in Love
NICOLA YOON	➤	Everything, Everything

GHOSTED IN L.A.
SINA GRACE

SINA GRACE IS A PROLIFIC graphic novelist and illustrator whose autobiographical works, *Not My Bag* and *Self-Obsessed*, are about living and working in Los Angeles. While he's also written such major comic books as *Uncanny X-Men*, his "slice of life" books about L.A. capture his hometown in the stylized way that only graphic pieces can.

He describes his newest comic-book series, *Ghosted in L.A.*, as "*Melrose Place* but with ghosts." In the story, a young woman finds community in an apartment complex populated with ghosts who lived and died in different eras. We sat down to talk about his comics at Alcove, an old house–turned–restaurant in Los Feliz.

Grace was born and raised in Santa Monica. "Nowadays I have to assert that it was rent-control Santa Monica because it's so different," he said. "People don't believe me when I say I grew up ten blocks from the beach, but in the late '80s and early '90s, it wasn't like now. We had a security guard at the front of the alleyway entrance. It's changed a lot. Santa Monica and Venice have both been dramatically affected by gentrification."

After college in Santa Cruz, Grace "spent a couple chapters in San Francisco" before returning to Los Angeles, although he's on the move often. "I travel a lot for work because I make comic books, so I get invited places, which provides an escape and a window to perspective," he said. "In L.A., we all live in our cars and our apartments or houses. The rent is crazy, but money affords you privacy here, much more so than in San Francisco or New York, so I think people can get stuck in their corners and not see what the rest of the nation is dealing with or thinking about." He considers that time spent outside of L.A. important to his work.

Comic books are his lifelong love. "As a kid, I super loved them and would get them at grocery stores, back when grocery stores still had comics," he said. "I'd go to my local comic shop, Hi De Ho Comics, which is still in business, and it's awesome." In high school, he interned at a comic-book company in Century City. "After school I'd take the bus and work there for a few hours a couple times a week. Summers, I'd work in the comic store and make zines and sell them at the register for a dollar. That was my unofficial start—having an insatiable desire to learn everything possible and then finding any and every avenue to explore. Which reminds me of another nice thing about living in Los Angeles: I was able to take the train to San Diego Comic-Con fifteen years ago, back when you could just get a day pass and check it out."

Grace's work varies between big-title comic books and his own, more personal stories. About transitioning between the two, he said, "It boils down to what material feels easy—easy in the sense that I'm inspired or excited to work on it. On top of that is the equation of what I like working on and what the audience responds to." In terms of taking the risk to tell his own stories, he added, "It took a really long time for me to realize that people didn't need a layer of fiction. Everyone was fine and excited to have it just be straight memoir. What makes me feel good about putting it out there is making it visually interesting. So with *Not My Bag*, for example, I knew it had to be gothic. My experience working in retail was really maddening, and I just felt that it lent itself to the gothic genre."

Hi De Ho Comics.

Ghosted in L.A. is a departure for Grace. This monthly series takes place in L.A. but is fictional, synthesizing various aspects of his work into one project. "I wanted to work with an editor at BOOM! Studios, Shannon Watters, who has amazing taste and an eye for how to move story in a compelling direction," he said. "I needed an editor who could find my blind spots and make me a better storyteller." With this project, he's getting into local lore. "Something I'm really interested in exploring is L.A.'s history before Hollywoodland," he said. "I'm absorbing information and letting what appeals to me feed into the art. There's no specific agenda beyond challenging myself to look at perspectives outside of what was a very male-dominated industry. For example, with the matriarch of the building, Agi, it's implied that her ex-husband was a Hollywood director who has moved on."

Another factor feeding into *Ghosted* is apartment living, which is not how many people think of L.A. "Growing up in apartment complexes, I've never lived in a house with a roommate. I wanted to examine that. Who are these people who live in these units where it's not conducive to raising a family? You're not admitting that these neighbors are your chosen family, but you are cohabitating with them. Some of the archetypes in the comics are people who live in my building currently, but more from an observational standpoint. I'll see someone smoking on the patio and wonder about their internal life.

"I'm taking these ghosts and using them as a way to teach myself more about L.A. outside of my own lens and my own life span."

Grace credits L.A. for having a strong local creative community: "What's super cool about this city is that it's not just film and TV that's here, but animation and books as well. I have a lot of friends who came here thinking they'd do comics and transitioned into animation, or people who are freelance graphic designers and also write TV, comic books, whatever. It's a little bit of everything. I'll hang out with my friend who is a freelance illustrator or go get happy hour with Cecil Castellucci. At the end of the day, it's really fun to talk to anybody and everybody about how they work and where the work comes from."

I turn my face to the window, and from where I lie on the bed, I can see the Hollywood sign. The Hollywood sign is a big disappointment. Surprise! It's totally tiny and boring. They completely misrepresent it in movies. I guess, like most things, it gets too many closeups so you can't see the whole picture.

— Cecil Castellucci, *Beige* (2007)

The other city—the remembered and imagined one—stretches west, past the sprawling ethnic neighborhoods where Koreans overlap with Salvadorans and Armenians back into Thais. It begins on the big-name crosstown boulevards lined with deco theaters, faded tropical motels, and restaurants with sentinel valets, and ends where the streets run into the ocean. But in this trench where the 110 sinks through downtown, that place is barely a memory. Here there is only the jam of the cars and the blank faces of the glass towers.

— IVY POCHODA, *Wonder Valley* (2017)

BOOK-LOVING EVENTS

LOS ANGELES TIMES FESTIVAL OF BOOKS

The Los Angeles Times Festival of Books (LATFOB) is one of the largest book festivals in the country. Drawing 150,000 attendees annually to the USC campus for two days of programming and exhibitions, typically in April, it proves how much Los Angeles is a literary city.

The weekend kicks off the Friday night before the festival opens with the L.A. Times Book Prizes, a gala ceremony recognizing the best writing from SoCal authors in categories including fiction, first fiction, biography, poetry, young adult literature, current interest, graphic novels, history, mystery/thriller, and science and technology. There's also the Innovator's Award, which "spotlights cutting-edge work to bring books, publishing, and storytelling into the future." Two final awards honor local writers: the Christopher Isherwood Prize for Autobiographical Prose, named for the late Santa Monica memoirist and fiction writer best known for *A Single Man*, and the Robert Kirsch Award, a lifetime-achievement honor for an author of the American West, named for the late literary editor of the *Los Angeles Times*.

Over the course of an LATFOB weekend, scores of authors speak on panels and sign books, dozens of poets perform readings, cookbook authors do demonstrations, publishers and booksellers host author signings at their booths, musicians perform, and a children's area buzzes with bookish kid-friendly happenings. Authors take advantage of the weekend to visit with friends, and readers find like-minded people and build community. And everyone goes home with a new stack of books to read.

MORE LITERARY EVENTS

➤ LAMBDA LITFEST • L.A.'s only LGBTQ literary festival, Lambda LitFest runs each September with dozens of events—slam poetry, storytelling, panels, readings, parties—held all around L.A.

➤ LIT CRAWL L.A. • Formerly based in North Hollywood, this bar crawl/popup reading series is now partnered with CicLAvia, an experiment that we hope works.

➤ LITFEST PASADENA • Each May, LitFest Pasadena hosts a weekend of free readings, panels, performances, and workshops all around the Playhouse District, especially including Vroman's and the Pasadena Playhouse. It's notable for its diversity, with something for everyone: kids, teens, poets, sci-fi fans, queer readers/writers, mystery lovers, and a broad range of ethnic and cultural groups.

➤ **LITLIT** • Inaugurated in 2019 and hosted by Hauser & Wirth and *LA Review of Books*, the free Little Literary Fair on the Hauser & Wirth gallery campus in DTLA celebrates independent publishing in Los Angeles and SoCal with publisher exhibits and a few art and culture panels.

➤ **PASADENA FESTIVAL OF WOMEN AUTHORS** • An all-day springtime event that brings together six nationally known women authors for talks and panels, with proceeds going to local literacy programs; a new offshoot is the quarterly, one-author-at-a-time Open Book series, featuring such authors as Amor Towles and Jacqueline Winspear.

➤ **PRINTED MATTER'S L.A. ART BOOK FAIR** • Held each spring at the Geffen Contemporary at MOCA, this is a three-day lovefest of small-press publishers, artists, collectives, paper geeks, galleries, antiquarian booksellers, collectors, and distributors.

➤ **SOUTHERN CALIFORNIA POETRY FESTIVAL** • More popularly called SoCalPoFest, this poetry festival is held each fall in a different SoCal city.

➤ **VERMIN ON THE MOUNT READING SERIES** • Writer Jim Ruland's irreverent, lively, occasional reading series is often hosted by Book Show in Highland Park, but it moves around.

➤ **WRITERS WEEK CONFERENCE** • Typically stretching longer than a calendar week, this is the longest-running free literary event in California, bringing both emerging and celebrated writers to UC Riverside every February; it attracts such big names as Margaret Atwood and Roxane Gay.

➤ **YALLWEST** • Founded by YA authors Melissa de la Cruz and Margaret Stohl, the free book fair features often-big-name YA and middle-grade writers and other creators taking part in panels, signings, giveaways, and games; it's held in Santa Monica, usually in early May.

Los Angeles remains the most photographed and least remembered city in the world.

— Norman M. Klein, *The History of Forgetting* (1997/2008)

SOMETHING UNEASY IN THE L.A. AIR

WRITERS ON THE WEATHER

We only have two kinds of weather in California, magnificent and unusual.

— JAMES M. CAIN,
The Baby in the Icebox and Other Short Fiction (1932)

The sun is a joke. Oranges can't titillate their jaded palates. Nothing can ever be violent enough to make taut their slack minds and bodies. They have been cheated and betrayed. They have slaved and saved for nothing.

— NATHANAEL WEST, *The Day of the Locust* (1939)

It's a hair too hot, as it always is in Los Angeles, where the sun has no mercy.

— MAGGIE NELSON, *The Argonauts* (2015)

There is something uneasy in the Los Angeles air, this afternoon, some unnatural stillness, some tension.

— JOAN DIDION, "Los Angeles Notebook" (1968)

The smog was heavy, my eyes were weeping from it, the sun was hot, the air stank, a regular hell is L.A.

— JACK KEROUAC, *The Dharma Bums* (1958)

The Santa Anas blew in hot from the desert, shriveling the last of the spring grass into whiskers of pale straw. Only the oleanders thrived, their delicate poisonous blooms, their dagger green leaves. We could not sleep in the hot dry nights, my mother and I.

— JANET FITCH, *White Oleander* (1999)

Los Angeles weather is the weather of catastrophe, of apocalypse, and, just as the reliably long and bitter winters of New England determine the way life is lived there, so the violence and the unpredictability of the Santa Ana affect the entire quality of life in Los Angeles, accentuate its impermanence, its unreliability. The wind shows us how close to the edge we are.

— JOAN DIDION,
"Los Angeles Notebook" (1968)

He'd say the weather was too good in California, and their lives were too easy, and they should see how the rest of the world lived.

— MAILE MELOY, *Liars and Saints* (2003)

In the eternal lazy morning of the Pacific, days slip away into months, months into years; the seasons are reduced to the faintest nuance by the great central fact of the sunshine; one might pass a lifetime, it seems, between two yawns, lying bronzed and naked in the sand.

— CHRISTOPHER ISHERWOOD,
"Los Angeles," *Horizon* magazine (1947)

Rain filled the gutters and splashed knee-high off the sidewalk. Big cops in slickers that shone like gun barrels had a lot of fun carrying giggling girls across the bad places. The rain drummed hard on the roof of the car and the burbank top began to leak. A pool of water formed on the floorboards for me to keep my feet in. It was too early in the fall for that kind of rain.

— RAYMOND CHANDLER, *The Big Sleep* (1939)

All day the heat had been barely supportable but at evening a breeze arose in the west, blowing from the heart of the setting sun and from the ocean, which lay unseen, unheard behind the scrubby foothills. It shook the rusty fringes of palm-leaf and swelled the dry sounds of summer, the frog-voices, the grating cicadas, and the ever-present pulse of music from the neighboring native huts.

— EVELYN WAUGH, *The Loved One* (1948)

A FEW MORE LITERARY LOCATIONS

THE BEVERLY HILLS HOTEL • From Gore Vidal to Eve Babitz, Bret Easton Ellis to Jackie Collins, writers have stayed here, dined here, and held meetings by the pool here. At press time, many are boycotting the Sunset Boulevard landmark because the current owner, the Sultan of Brunei, had announced plans to adhere to Sharia law, which calls for the persecution of homosexuals. Time will tell how this shakes out.

CHARLES BUKOWSKI BUNGALOW • Now a protected L.A. Historic-Cultural Monument, this modest bungalow at 5124 De Longpre Ave. was home to Bukowski in the years when he worked at the post office and transitioned to becoming a famous poet, novelist, drunk, and ne'er-do-well. His favorite liquor store, the iconic Pink Elephant, is but a few blocks away on Western.

LUMMIS HOME & GARDENS

One of L.A.'s earliest and most influential writers and editors was Charles Fletcher Lummis, who walked from Cincinnati to L.A. in 1884 for a job at the *Los Angeles Times*, a publicity stunt that made him famous by the time he arrived. He bought land on the edge of the Arroyo in what is now Highland Park, spent a dozen years building an incredible house by hand out of Arroyo rock, helped grow L.A.'s Arts & Crafts movement, founded a magazine called *Land of Sunshine*, for which he hired such notables as Jack London and Charlotte Perkins Gilman, and wrote his own essays and poetry. The house he called El Alisal (Place of the Sycamore Trees) is now a city park and is open to the public on weekends.

UPTON SINCLAIR HOUSE •

Activist writer Sinclair, who won a Pulitzer in 1943 for his novel *The Jungle*, moved to this house at 464 N. Myrtle Ave. in Monrovia in 1942. He relocated from Pasadena in search of quiet for his writing, and he lived, wrote, and ran for political office from here until 1966. The National Historic Landmark is a private residence, so please don't knock on the door, but do stop by to admire the 1924 Mediterranean building.

VILLA CARLOTTA

This grand, ornate Spanish Colonial apartment building at 5959 Franklin Ave. in Hollywood has been shabby for more of its storied life than it has been glamorous, which just added to its charm. Writer William Saroyan lived here, as did the famed gossip columnist Louella Parsons. The Historic-Cultural Monument was recently restored and is now a swank residential hotel for stays of thirty days or longer.

ZANE GREY ESTATE

The phenomenally prolific writer Grey, who specialized in Westerns and wrote more than ninety books, and his wife, Dolly, who was his editor and ran his business affairs, bought this 1907 Mediterranean Revival mansion on Altadena's "Millionaire's Row" in 1920, and it stayed in the family for half a century. The sprawling property, at 396 E. Mariposa St., remains in private hands and is on the National Register of Historic Places.

Delaney couldn't feel bad for long, not up here where the night hung close round him and the crickets thundered and the air off the Pacific crept up the hills to drive back the lingering heat of the day. There were even stars, a cluster here or there fighting through the wash of light pollution that turned the eastern and southern borders of the night yellow, as if a whole part of the world had gone rancid. To the north and east lay the San Fernando Valley, a single endless plane of parallel boulevards, houses, mini-malls and streetlights, and to the south lay the rest of Los Angeles, ad infinitum.

— T. C. BOYLE, *Tortilla Curtain* (1995)

The Twentieth Century is made in Los Angeles.
The stars amass and suffer its novelties.

— DAVID ROWBOTHAM, *Poems for America* (2002)

ACKNOWLEDGMENTS

READ ME, LOS ANGELES would not exist without the hard work of everyone at Prospect Park. I could not have had a better team to collaborate with, and they made my work so much better for their insights and suggestions. Thanks to Colleen, Katelyn, Caitlin, Julianne, and Dorie; to copyeditor Leilah Bernstein and proofreader Margery L. Schwartz; to photographer Shahin Ansari; to cover illustrator Kate Wong; and especially to Amy Inouye for the beautiful design and layout.

My agent, Dara Hyde, walked me through the book's inception to its completion, and I am so grateful for her guidance, support, and constant push to make my writing better.

I don't think I would have ever dreamed of writing about literary tourism had it not been for the late Dr. Pamela Corpron Parker, my advisor and friend. Her academic specialty in literary tourism taught me that other people also love to explore new places through the lens of an author or book they love, and it gave a name to my enduring passion. Her specialty also led me to Dr. Shirley Foster, my graduate advisor and another expert in literary tourism. While this book is different from their output, I hope they see their fingerprints in my essays.

My life in Los Angeles is inextricably entwined with the Last Bookstore in its first decade. So much in my essays for this book was formed by the people I met there, from my coworkers, to our customers, to the authors who came for events. The constant access to a wealth of L.A. books played a huge part in my research. My life as a bookseller has also brought me so many friends in both the local and worldwide bookselling communities, and I am grateful for their friendship and support.

To the authors who gave their time to sit and discuss their work and this city, my ceaseless gratitude. Michael, Jerry, Luis, David, Naomi, Dana, Aimee, Liska, Michael, Amber, Francesca, and Sina—all of you shared insight into this city and how writing is a way to understand it. Special thanks to Mike Sonksen, not only for your advice as I planned my writing but for the piece you contributed.

My friends have been so forgiving of my diminished availability as I dedicated my time to reading, researching, and writing. Thanks especially to Lisa, Kara, Sarah, Carolyn, Liska, Evangeline, Jen, Matt, and the Brians. The listening ears, advice, company, and myriad other shows of support have made my life all the better.

Finally, to my family: Thank you for never trying to talk me out of writing and into something more "practical." Your support buoys me every day. I am so grateful for a family of engineers who love to read, who read to me daily when I was a child, who took me to the library (too often if we go by the fines I incurred), and who have told me constantly that they believe in me. Let's hope I've made you proud—especially you, Eleanor.

— KATIE ORPHAN

Katie Orphan is the manager of Libreria L.A.; before that, she worked at the Last Bookstore for a decade. She writes the recurring feature "Drinking with the Ghosts" for the Los Angeles Review of Books *and is the author of the Last Bookstore's guide to downtown Los Angeles.*

A city no worse than others, a city rich and vigorous and full of pride, a city lost and beaten and full of emptiness. It all depends on where you sit and what your own private score is. I didn't have one. I didn't care. I finished the drink and went to bed.

— RAYMOND CHANDLER, *The Long Goodbye* (1953)

INDEX